W9-CEH-062

A North Country Almanac

A North Country Almanac

REFLECTIONS OF AN OLD-SCHOOL CONSERVATIONIST IN A MODERN WORLD

Thomas C. Bailey

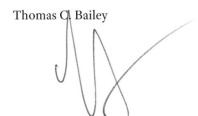

MICHIGAN STATE UNIVERSITY PRESS | *East Lansing*

⊗ The paper used in this publication meets the minimum requirements
of ANSI/NISO z39.48-1992 (R 1997) (Permanence of Paper).

MICHIGAN STATE UNIVERSITY PRESS
East Lansing, Michigan 48823-5245

The Dave Dempsey Environmental Series

Printed in China.

27   26   25   24   23   22   21   20   19   18   1   2   3   4   5   6   7   8   9   10

LIBRARY OF CONGRESS CATALOGING-IN-PUBLICATION DATA IS AVAILABLE
ISBN 978-1-61186-286-7 (cloth)
ISBN 978-1-60917-566-5 (PDF)

Book design by Charlie Sharp, Sharp Des!gns, East Lansing, MI
Cover design by Erin Kirk New
Front and back cover images as well as all interior images are ©2016 and used courtesy
of the artist, Heidi Amenda Marshall (heidiamarshall.com). All rights reserved.

Michigan State University Press is a member of the Green Press Initiative and is
committed to developing and encouraging ecologically responsible publishing
practices. For more information about the Green Press Initiative and the use
of recycled paper in book publishing, please visit *www.greenpressinitiative.org*.

Visit Michigan State University Press at *www.msupress.org*

Contents

Foreword

Gloria Whelan

TOM BAILEY HAS BEEN PROTECTING THE LAND SINCE HE WAS SEVENTEEN years old. That was the year he appeared as a federal witness before the U.S. Senate Interior Committee in support of protecting Michigan's Isle Royale National Park as federal wilderness.

Thoreau wrote, "A man has not seen a thing who has not felt it." Tom's feel for the outdoors is bred in the bones. His father was a wildlife biologist. His childhood was spent in the outdoors, camping, hunting, and fishing. He remembers how moved he was at the sight of his first eagle. He was five years old.

Bailey believes the preservation of the land is not just for the conservationist, it's for everyone. We can't all tramp through forests, but we should be able to. Wallace Stegner says, "Something will have gone out of us as a people if we ever let the remaining wilderness be destroyed. . . . We simply need that wild country available to us, even if we never do more than drive to its edge and look in."

What Tom knows is that every day is a day of battle for the conservationist. Tom wears the dog tags of his father, a veteran of World War II, and the dog tags of his son, a veteran of battles in Afghanistan. Tom, himself, is every bit a fighter, not only for the acquisition and preservation of land, but someone with the courage to say what he thinks when opposing environmental piety.

Isn't hunting antienvironmental, what with guns and the killing of animals? Absolutely not, Tom says, pointing out that it was the hunters and anglers who first recognized and spoke of the importance of preserving the environment. It is their license fees that go toward the purchase and care of land not only for themselves, but for us all.

Aren't property taxes all good since they support the government's work in preserving land? Wait a moment, Tom says. What about the people who live in small homes on a lake where the building of high-value houses is escalating taxes so that owners of a modest home can no longer afford to keep it?

The amazing thing about Tom Bailey is that he has the genius to bring together, over the cause of conservation, people of all persuasions. The Board of the Little Traverse Conservancy includes builders and developers, scientists and environmentalists. He tells us he has even had members who work together on the board, and when away from the board, sue one another!

This art of bringing people together is needed more than ever in these days of contention. A recent cartoon in the *New Yorker* makes gentle fun of those who have no clue about nature. A couple of "city folk" are sitting pensively on a hill with the land all about them. One asks the other, "What time does the outdoors close?" These essays give an insight into how Tom Bailey conveys the sense of love for the land as well as the urgency of the need to protect it.

The essays delight and instruct. They first came into our lives nearly thirty years ago, when my husband and I left the city to live where our hearts were—in northern Michigan. When I-75 was in the process of construction just a short distance from our summer cabin on the Au Sable River, we asked a realtor to show us some property. We visited several sites. Finally he said, "I have a place that probably wouldn't interest you. It's at the end of the world." We bought it the next day.

Oxbow Lake is thirty acres surrounded by woods. The cabin we built was the only human habitation on the lake. One evening a friend came to visit. After a long silent time of looking at the lake he said, "You ought to put a conservation easement on this property." We didn't know what that was. We approached the Little Traverse Conservancy. Many years later we moved back to the city, but because of the easement, which was later transferred to the newly formed Grand Traverse Conservancy that now covered our area, the family who owns the property enjoys the same view we did of a pristine lake embraced by a shore with nothing on it but trees.

It was at the time of establishing our conservancy that Tom's essays entered our lives. We enjoyed them so much I urged Tom to publish them so a larger audience could be inspired. It was a long wait, but here in this book are words that reflect a life given in equal parts to the celebration of nature and to its preservation.

Prelude

ONE OF MY MOST FUNDAMENTAL BELIEFS IS THAT WALT WHITMAN WAS stating a truth when he wrote, "Now I see the secret of making the best persons: it is to grow in the open air, and eat and sleep with the earth." I believe that the experience of living and growing and eating and sleeping outdoors makes us better people. I don't advocate that we should do this all the time—I wouldn't want to always live at a campsite, nor would I suggest that humanity should "go back" to what most regard as a primitive lifestyle. But I would suggest that a certain amount of outdoor experience is good for people. It builds character, self-esteem, self-reliance, and the ability to deal with what life and the world offer.

That's more than just an opinion. Much research has been done on this sort of thing, ranging from the Outward Bound experience among wealthy suburbanite youngsters to outdoor training and survival trips for business executives to outdoor programs directed at disadvantaged youth and juvenile delinquents. Convincing evidence tells us that outdoor activity can have a very significant, positive and lasting effect on the development of individuals and their ability to adapt and function in a variety of contexts. It seems especially beneficial for people who live in dysfunctional situations—broken families, alcoholic households, and so on—to spend time in the healing hands of nature which is consistently true to itself, and which does not play favorites with the people who choose to travel in the wilds.

I can say with certainty that my life has been made vastly better because of the time I spent outdoors and the things I learned there. The living earth, what we often call the world of nature, has been my refuge, my retreat, and my haven.

I BELIEVE THAT IF MORE CHILDREN COULD SPEND MORE TIME IN THE NATURAL world, they would have fewer problems. I believe that there would be less helplessness and hopelessness and homelessness in our society if more people were able to spend more time learning and growing outdoors.

I believe in the rightness and goodness of nature to the very depths of my being. I've seen the healing and powerful regenerative effect that nature has had on me and on others, and the goodness and rightness of this power is something I know to be true.

I also believe that our American culture has a special link to the outdoors, and that if we sacrifice too much of our wild lands and outdoor heritage on the altar of short-term profits, we will have sold out the most important thing that defines who we are as Americans: the living land that shaped our culture, our people, and our selves.

I've been speaking out passionately for the protection of natural land since the ripe old age of seventeen, when I appeared before the U.S. Senate Interior Committee on behalf of protecting Michigan's Isle Royale National Park as federal wilderness. I lobbied in Michigan to secure support for this and other wilderness protection efforts in the state legislature, the governor's office, and the state natural resources commission.

Involvement in conservation came naturally to me. My father spent thirty-seven years as a wildlife biologist with the Michigan Department of Natural Resources. I grew up hunting, fishing, and camping with my dad and with our entire family as we enjoyed trips around the country in an early-model tent camper and, later, backpacking and canoe trips.

I've always tended to follow through on my interests in depth, and so in addition to working on wilderness protection for Isle Royale National Park, I also served two summers as a park ranger there. I spent another summer in the National Park Service with time split between Isle Royale and Grand Portage National Monument in northern Minnesota. I've also been a member of the

National Ski Patrol and a fishing guide—I guess I like to work in areas where most people like to play.

I'm doing that now, as executive director of the Little Traverse Conservancy, a nonprofit land conservation organization in northern Michigan. Our mission is to protect natural and scenic areas by acquiring land and conservation easements, and by sponsoring environmental education programs which teach children about the outdoors in the outdoors. It's a simple and straightforward mission, and a very inclusive organization. We don't require that prospective board, staff, or organizational members adhere to any particular orthodoxy.

I am especially proud of the fact that there's no litmus test to be a part of the Conservancy. Some of our area's most notorious environmentalists, as well as the most notorious developers, serve on our board of trustees. In fact, we've had situations where board members were actively suing one another outside our board room over other matters, but still agreed when seated around our table that the Conservancy's conservation programs and techniques are both appropriate and necessary.

The Little Traverse Conservancy's open philosophy is quite consistent with my own. I consider myself a former political activist, not a current one. I'm not on the front lines anymore and do not wish to be. So, like the Conservancy, I say: feel how you want to feel about such issues as nuclear power, the Endangered Species Act, hitting baby seals over the head, or whatever. As long as you believe in conservationists putting their money where their mouth is—and where their heart is—to protect land, there's room for you under what we like to call our "big tent."

That's not to say that issues like hunting, nuclear power, and such aren't important; they clearly are. But there are appropriate times and places to fight over such things, and in the meantime, I think we should all rally together around the big-picture issues that we have in common. After making progress on those, we can proceed to the more detailed and divisive issues. I have come to believe that there is not necessarily one right view of these issues. We need to remember that nature teaches us that everything is connected to everything else. Nothing is black and white.

Prior to working for the Conservancy, I spent six years with the Michigan Department of Natural Resources. I licensed hazardous waste haulers and inspected hazardous waste treatment, storage, and disposal facilities. I also administered state and federal grants for water pollution control projects, primarily consisting of municipal sewer systems and wastewater treatment plants.

My environmental ethic developed over time. I learned early on from my father that it is not enough to just enjoy things like hunting and fishing—you also need to give something back. I've been not only a fisherman, but also a guide. I've been an enthusiastic park visitor, and an equally enthusiastic national park ranger.

I enjoy sharing the beauty and wonder of great natural land with others. Along with being a skier, I joined the ski patrol; and today, along with working at a land conservancy, I also serve on the National Land Trusts Council of the Land Trust Alliance.

The outdoors is my passion. As a youngster, I spent as much time as possible outside. I loved to play in the woods and especially along the shoreline of the Great Lakes—in fact, I did most of my growing up along the shore of Lake Superior.

My earliest outdoor memories include following my dad through pheasant cover. He carried a well-worn Marlin pump 20-gauge which his father had used before him, and he carried a contagious enthusiasm and love for the outdoors. Even though my legs would tire, I loved following Dad on a hunt. I thrilled when a bird went up, loved the smell of gunpowder after the shot, and would usually ask for a pheasant's tail feather to put in my hat or to use for a pen. Dad involved me in the cleaning of the birds, showing me their feathers and also their internal workings. I was amazed to watch him open a pheasant's crop and show me what the bird had been eating. Dad always taught me about the need to follow hunting limits to assure a continuing supply of game.

Pheasant hunting gave way to grouse hunting when we moved from southern Michigan to the Upper Peninsula, and when I was old enough to carry a gun on a hunt, it was the country around Gwinn, Michigan, where I spent most of my time. Grouse, deer, bear, and other game were abundant. I hunted with my father, with a couple of very close friends, and sometimes alone. I practiced shooting after school, and would go on a camping trip whenever I had the chance.

Backpacking was introduced to me by my uncle Wayne, who held not only a deep love of nature but also a gift for making and working with equipment. It was he who introduced me to the wonderful world of specialized lightweight camping gear, and I've been a sort of gadget junkie ever since. Dad, Uncle Wayne, and I hiked the length of Isle Royale during the summer of my sixteenth year. Somewhere along the Greenstone Ridge Trail, my plans to pursue a career in land conservation became solidified. I had vowed since age nine that I would be a national park ranger someday, and on that first trip to Isle Royale, I determined that protecting wild country through a career with the National Park Service was what I wanted to do.

But things change. After getting my degree in park and recreation resources from Michigan State University, I married a woman who was obviously not going to be your average ranger wife following me from park to park. Career plan B took me, quite happily, to the Michigan Department of Natural Resources, where I learned a lot about bureaucracy and about working with people. I learned about organizations, positive and negative, and I learned that I really wanted to get out of the regulatory system and back into hands-on conservation. When they wouldn't let me get into public affairs work because of my lack of a degree in English or journalism, I left the DNR and sought refuge in Michigan's North Country. I found the perfect niche in my job with the Little Traverse Conservancy.

MY POLITICS TEND TOWARD THE CONSERVATIVE SIDE. A LOT OF FOLKS THINK that conservatism and environmentalism are incompatible, but I see that as political myth and the product of the inconsistencies of American politics. I took a lot of grief from environmentalist friends when I voted for Nixon in 1972, yet he was the president who created the Environmental Protection Agency and whose administration supported and implemented some of the most progressive environmental legislation in history.

I believe that environmental conservation is, in essence, a conservative cause. It represents a certain resistance to change that tends to be seen as typically conservative, and it involves placing trust in people to manage their own affairs and shared resources wisely. I'm skeptical about too much environmental regulation because I've been part of the regulatory bureaucracy and I understand many of its shortcomings.

While many of my environmental friends and colleagues are heavily dependent upon the regulatory paradigms—seeing the only way to a sustainable future as being through heavy restrictions and regulations on behavior—I tend to lean in the opposite direction. I believe that all humans seek fulfillment and productive living in harmony with the earth. People will find the right way if given the time. I believe that the way out of the current environmental crisis is to unleash our creativity, not bottle it up. This is not to say that I believe in a technical fix for every problem—in fact, I think we are too heavily dependent upon technology at this particular juncture. But ingenuity is more than technology—it can involve the "less is more" concept.

I look forward to the implementation of what one might call a "postregulatory" paradigm. Just as we have emerged into postindustrial society and the information age, I believe that we can develop alternatives to the coercive regulatory model for modifying human behavior. I believe that incentives, reward structures, and such can be modified so that negative regulation will be replaced by positive incentive. Writers ranging from Paul Hawken to Jack Kemp have made impressive arguments about this exciting possibility.

And so here I am. In the footsteps of my father, I'm working to protect what I love about the outdoors and to help more people enjoy it. In the footsteps of my son, I see a track that will lead ahead and beyond where I am able to go. As a middle-aged man, I am steadily more aware of the fact that winter will one day come without a spring that I shall ever see. The fact that I'm becoming more and more comfortable with that thought is, perhaps, as much a reflection of my belief in nature as it is my advancing years; nature teaches that everything changes, and that everything is always in the process of becoming something else.

These essays represent snapshots of the views and experiences I have had over a period of many years. They are offered in hope that they will provide amusement, inspiration, and maybe a little fun. I have been blessed with a wonderful life and wonderful experience because of conservation and the outdoors, and if in sharing these thoughts and feelings I can help others to have a richer experience of nature and a greater appreciation for natural land, then my wish will be fulfilled and my goal achieved.

PART 1

Beginnings

Dusk Dreams at Minnehaha

Inspired by Eagles

WHEN PEOPLE ASK HOW I CAME TO WORK IN THE FIELD OF CONSERVATION, I have been known to respond, with a half-smile, that it is because I saw a bald eagle when I was about five years old.

I have vivid memories of that first eagle sighting, as I do of forcing my parents to stop the car so that I could take pictures of an eagle's nest we encountered on a family vacation. I've never been able to take my eyes off an eagle when one was in sight, and I've been privileged to see them many, many times.

I've seen eagles fishing on lakes in the western Upper Peninsula. What a treat it was to watch the great birds soaring over the water, then diving down to snatch a fish from the water and fly off to a convenient tree or nest! I've also been fortunate enough to live near eagles—there's a pair nesting about five miles, as the eagle flies, from my office. We have another pair of eagles living near Cross Village, where our family has a small rustic house on the Lake Michigan shore. Several times, while eating breakfast or looking out the window, I have seen the great birds drifting on wind currents along the bluff, fifty feet over the water but barely ten feet above our front yard and close enough that I could see the movement of every muscle that controls those powerful wings and talons.

I recently watched a big, mature eagle make an incredible grab of a large fish from the waters of Lake Michigan. It was a windy day, blowing hard out of the northwest. The bird was soaring in lazy circles over the beach, at least one or two thousand feet up in the air. Suddenly, it veered out over the water and into what must have been a half-mile-long dive. Never swerving from its course, while still a good three hundred feet from its target the eagle flashed its talons and adjusted its wings for the drag against the wind. The waves were pretty big—three to four feet high at least, with foaming whitecaps. But the bird kept on and snatched up a fish that was large enough for me to see from half a mile away and, laboring with its great wings, lifted its prize up above the waves and flew back to a tree to enjoy its meal. What a wonderful privilege it was for me to see!

THOUGH IT MAY SEEM SUPERSTITIOUS TO SOME, I HAVE FOUND THROUGH MY experience that eagles generally bring some sort of message or meaning when they appear. For example, the morning after the last Conservancy board meeting of 1991, I was mired in detail. There were year-end projects to wrap up, what with the tax year ending and books to close, and the phone was ringing constantly and people were waiting to see me. Our office construction project was at its dirty worst with drywall dust everywhere, unfinished materials lying about, and incessant noise from saws, sanders, drills, and tromping feet. The day was shaping up to be one of "those." I sank into my chair, sighed heavily, and rolled my eyes as I thought about the day to come. Seeing movement out the window, I turned my head and was startled to see a bald eagle soaring on the wind less than five hundred feet away.

The great bird was passing over the north end of Round Lake, headed toward Little Traverse Bay, no doubt to look for fish. With broad, powerful wings set, it coursed slowly and majestically off to the west, borne by a stiff breeze. The eagle was in sight for only five or six seconds, but it changed my entire day and my temporarily mired-down attitude.

The aggravations associated with paperwork, construction, and phone calls, melted suddenly away and left the real purpose of my work directly before me: protecting the wild beauty and natural freedom of the North Country. The stacks piled high on my desk were no longer just paperwork—they were about eagles, trees, fish, lakes, and the kinds of areas where eagles can live and grow and raise their young. They were about the people of today and tomorrow who will be better off for having wild country close at hand. They were about all the people who didn't see the magnificent bird soar overhead, but who gladly and generously support our efforts just so they can know that somewhere the eagles have a home.

Ends and means snapped sharply into perspective as I understood the message the eagle brought. I shook my head thinking of the many moments in my life when the sighting of an eagle accompanied something momentous or significant, and silently thanked the great bird for the newest insight.

Four months later, I was also preoccupied. My son was hospitalized with an unknown ailment. I was headed to the hospital as Jane and I traded shifts, each staying with John on alternate nights. I drove around the curve of M-119 past Spring Lake with a furrowed brow, but still caught a movement out of the corner of my eye and saw the unmistakable silhouette and slow, rhythmic wingbeat of an eagle rising up above the lake and beginning to circle. I could not help but take the eagle's presence as a sign of sorts and had the feeling that the appearance of the eagle somehow confirmed that everything would be all right with John.

My spirits were buoyed as I arrived at the hospital for a day that would turn out to be the most frightening in my life. Later that day, I watched in an unbelieving, dreadfully helpless state of shock as my son stopped breathing. I felt as though I had stopped breathing, too. I yelled for the nurse as the world seemed to fade into a haze. I faintly hear the code call that brought dozens of doctors, nurses, pulmonary specialists, and others rushing in to help. I stood numbly nearby with Jane, as the team went to work to save the precious three-year-old boy who looked so very small and lifeless on the big hospital bed. Then, I faintly heard encouraging words from the room and finally the news that John was recovering and should have no ill effects from his close call. We felt great relief, but also the sort of fear and numbness that only sets in after such an incident.

I didn't think about the eagle again until the next day, when I finally headed home for a rest. Passing Spring Lake, I looked out over where the eagle had flown two days before. It seemed as though a century had passed. I thought about the way my spirits had surged when I saw the eagle, and remembered thinking after I saw the great bird that everything would be all right. It had ended well, indeed, but there had been no inkling of what John and Jane and I would have to endure before it was over.

Just as the eagle four months earlier had prompted me to reflect on the things that are most important in my work, I had now been prompted to think about the importance of my family. Our preciousness to each other had been vividly demonstrated. I was also reminded of how fortunate we were to have a first-rate hospital in the North with dedicated people who could provide life-saving help when needed. And I was reminded, as well, of the many generous people whose giving makes that all-important facility possible.

These two visits from eagles, just four months apart but on very different occasions, jarred me into looking at things anew.

No eagle flew overhead as I made my way wearily home from the hospital that day. But I have no doubt that an eagle will appear again at a special moment to help me see what I need to see. Eagles have brought many lessons to me, and if I am lucky, and if I listen and look, they will bring me many more. Thank you, my beautiful soaring friends, for helping me to learn, to grow and to understand.

(1999)

A Yooper Kid Goes to Washington

THE EARLY 1970S WERE A TIME OF ENVIRONMENTAL ACTIVISM AND AWARE-ness. Earth Day and the dawning of what would come to be known as the "environmental movement" brought issues like air and water pollution and other human impacts on the earth to the fore.

As the son of a wildlife biologist, I suppose I was ahead of the curve when it came to environmental awareness. I had grown up fishing, hunting, camping, and learning about the outdoors in the venerable conservation tradition of Theodore Roosevelt and Aldo Leopold. The environment was nothing new to me, and I remember talking with my dad, who said in a somewhat bemused fashion that he was glad that people were finally waking up to the fact that there was such a thing as the natural environment.

I had first backpacked in Michigan's Isle Royale National Park in 1969, and had grown to love the park's beautiful island wilderness. I was taken aback when I read in our local newspaper, the *Marquette Mining Journal*, that a proposal by the National Park Service would exclude substantial areas of the park from designation as wilderness under the federal Wilderness Act of 1964. It seemed to me that if there was ever a place for designated wilderness in the national park system, the interior of an island in the middle of Lake Superior was it.

Learning of a public meeting to be held on the matter, I headed over to the science building on the campus of Northern Michigan University, which was conveniently just a quarter mile or so from our house. I listened to a presentation by Doug Scott, then with the Wilderness Society in Washington, D.C., about how citizens can make a difference. I was spellbound. Doug made a passionate case for wilderness designation for Isle Royale, and also for citizens who believed it right to rise up and oppose a Park Service plan that would have left huge gaps in designated wilderness and would leave the park open to inappropriate development and exploitation.

Along with Doug Scott's inspirational presentation I learned about the Michigan Student Environmental Coalition, which was quite active in those days in Michigan environmental issues. Walt Pomeroy, the executive director of MSEC, became another mentor and a friend. I signed up as a member of MSEC, and also signed up to work with a group of people to create an alternative to the Park Service's proposal, which we thought was far from adequate.

Over the next year and more, I worked locally to help create the Citizens Alternative Proposal. I learned about writing to my congressman, lobbying state legislators to support our proposal, and working to gain the support of Michigan's governor. I was only a high school kid, but I teamed up with the MSEC's college students and a group who seemed to me like "old folks" to form the Northern Michigan Wilderness Coalition, and the movement grew.

We worked for wilderness on a number of levels, including designation of wilderness areas across the UP on state and federal land, but my primary focus remained Isle Royale. Hearings were scheduled in Washington, D.C., and I was lucky enough to get the Sierra Club to pay my way to Washington to testify.

So it was that my first commercial jet flight took me on a DC-9 from Marquette to Detroit, then a Boeing 727 from Detroit to Washington in June 1972. I was seventeen years old.

From the time I left the runway at Marquette County Airport, I was in awe. Jet flight was new to me. Departing Detroit and passing over Lake Erie, I saw firsthand how terrible the water quality had become in the lake, with large areas of unnaturally colored water and gunk. And in Washington, I not only saw the Capitol and the House and Senate office buildings, I went inside to take my case to my congressman and senator.

I spent time at the Wilderness Society preparing my testimony for the Senate Interior Committee's Public Land Subcommittee, headed then by Idaho senator Frank Church. Doug Scott was a teacher, mentor, and friend. I learned more about the legislative process than I could have imagined, and through direct experience saw Congress at work. I had a meeting with an assistant secretary of the interior and learned a lot about the executive branch's inner workings. It wasn't Civics 101; it was Civics on Steroids.

Over the next few years, I remained involved and was finally rewarded when our proposal was approved and then signed into law in 1976. I met some wonderful people in the environmental/conservation/wilderness movement at the state and federal levels, including such notables as the organizers of the first Environmental Teach-In at University of Michigan and Ernie Dickerman, progenitor of the Eastern Wilderness movement. I worked with members of Congress, senators, committee staff in both houses, and people in the National Park Service. At the state level, I met legislators, Executive Office staff, natural resources commissioners, and others. I worked with some of the most notable early activists in the Michigan environmental movement in the 1970s and learned and learned and learned.

Because I attended Michigan State University, I could jump aboard a bus and for thirty-five cents ride down to the state capitol to work on legislation and administrative policy. I was a regular at the MSEC office and served as Lansing representative for UP wilderness advocates.

I returned to Washington when the legislation passed by the Senate was considered on the House side, and remember the look of disbelief on the face of my Organic Chemistry professor when I told him that on the day of his final exam, I was scheduled to testify before the House Interior Committee. He laughed, and said that he'd never heard that excuse before. No, I said, this is for real! He didn't believe me. I arranged to have one of the committee staff members write, on congressional letterhead, that I was scheduled to testify, and so received grudging permission to take the final in his office, personally supervised by the Professor Himself. As I recall, I squeaked by with a grade of 1.5.

I learned more than I could have dreamed about how our government works and how, as Doug Scott said, things can change when people say, with determination, "There ought to be a law!" Public Law 94-567, a bill designating wilderness areas in a number of national parks and monuments, shows that people—even a kid from Michigan's Upper Peninsula—can make a difference.

(2016)

An Environmentalist Looks at Fifty

REMEMBER THE LATE 1960S AND EARLY 1970S, WHEN THE MODERN ENVIRON-mental movement took off? Heady times they were, pitting (some of us thought) the forces of good against the forces of evil. Greedy industrialists, shameless polluters, and cold-hearted rapists of the environment were finally challenged by a long-haired, flannel-shirted, and boot-clad generation who knew beyond the shadow of a doubt what was good for nature and good for humanity. My Vibram soles tromped in unison with others in the fight for the environment.

It seems like more than three decades have passed [and two more since this was written], because a funny thing has happened since the early days: we grew up. We discovered that things cannot so easily be described in black and white as they can in shades of grey. We learned that most everybody falls somewhere into the complicated no-one's land where there is no simple distinction between environmental innocence and guilt. Many of us have grown more conservative, though some of our number would vigorously (and rightly) disagree. Hence I can speak only for myself, but my observations are these.

Our movement, like ourselves, has come of age. Gone are the carefree days of throwing stones (figuratively for most of us, but literally for a few) at the bad actors in the drama and feeling smug and self-righteous about ourselves. We've traded our youthful rose-colored glasses for a middle-aged view of things that brings with it the uncomfortable kind of introspection that reveals us as more part of "the problem" than we had expected. Gone for the most part are the hippies and eco-freaks of yore. We've traded our flannel shirts for pinpoint-oxford and our hiking boots for frighteningly yuppified Topsiders. Many of the boiler-room environmental groups through which we worked to save the world have been dissolved, and in place of midnight work sessions to get out publications with names like *Earth Beat,* we have now embraced cars, kids, and consumerism.

We catch ourselves firing up our suburban gas grills and realize that our special-occasion beef was fattened up on public land. We'd gladly pay more for that meat, we tell ourselves, if the government would just raise those damned grazing fees. We'd welcome a fifty cents per gallon gas tax, too, knowing full well that we'd simply pay the extra money and burn just as much as we do today in the vehicles stored in our one- two-, and, increasingly, three-car garages. Welcome to self-awareness, kids: we're seeing shades of gray in more than just our thinning hair.

THERE ARE A FEW HOLDOUTS FROM THE OLD DAYS, STEREOTYPED TODAY as cotton-clad, bike-riding recycling fanatics who head the neighborhood hazardous waste watch. Some of our former number have split off into ecofeminism and the politics thereof, others to the New Age movement, and others into something called deep ecology. Some simply "died and went to the suburbs," as the saying goes, content to become what they once would have considered to be part of the problem.

But most of us, even though we have become more "middle class" than we envisioned in 1972, have by no means repudiated the ideals to which we dedicated so much of our youth. We've made progress toward solving many of the problems we identified in the sixties in our new roles as officeholders, corporate staffers, board members, and some of us still through conservation organizations. The impact of our work, and the awareness we created, shows. Witness the astounding progress of Lake Erie from the symbolic cesspool of the sixties to an encouraging, continuing recovery. Witness the extent to which people know about and think about their environment. Today, clean air and clean water are major issues, which they definitely were not in 1962. We've made substantial progress, and can take heart from what we've accomplished.

Now that we've won some major progress and cut pollutant discharges to an astounding degree, we're left to wrestle with the more subtle, difficult, and troubling problems that hit closer to home as we environmental activists begin to turn fifty. And we're facing those choices as middle-aged parents with a "comfortable" standard of living—very different circumstances than when we founded and became immersed in the Movement.

Quite a few of us remain suspended somewhere between the still-active ecofreaks and the former activists who surrendered to suburbia. A few years back, I thought that I was different—a 1970s activist who twenty years later was still focused almost exclusively on conservation. Then, I read a survey conducted to profile the "typical CEO of a non-profit conservation organization." The profile was that of a white male aged about forty to forty-five who earned $30,000–$45,000 working for a government agency but took a pay cut to leave and head a nonprofit. He has been in his job for five to seven years and got interested in conservation at an early age as a result of being inspired by a family member or friend who had a profound impact on the choice of a career in conservation. It's my story almost exactly, and another middle-aged wakeup call: I am not as different as I thought.

We may be conservation group CEOs or the more numerous environmental careerists who still work for the National Park Service, state resource

management agencies, or local planning commissions. Others work for the flagship environmental groups which survive—the Sierra Club, National Wildlife Federation, and others. Many of us focus more on private conservation efforts than the government with which we've become disillusioned in record numbers. In general, as the members of the Environmental Generation turn fifty, we're more diverse in our interests and perspectives than we were in "the good old days," and many, though by no means all, are now more conservative, to use a word we would not have applied to ourselves in the early 1970s.

But while we see things differently, we also see different things. The Statement of Chief Seattle, which we quoted so passionately, turns out to have been written by a screenwriter. The writer didn't intend for it to become a hoax—he was just trying and succeeding at creating a passionate speech for a poignant moment on film. The statement became a rallying cry for us because it fit our purpose exactly and we felt no need to ask further questions about it. Therein lies a lesson, typical of what we're learning as we age: things are not always as they appear, and innocent mistakes are mistakes nonetheless. On the brighter side, however—the side reflecting the idealism that we retain in spite of our more settled ways—the lesson also teaches us that we can learn as much from fiction and fantasy as we can from dry, supposedly objective reality. Plans and facts are okay, but there's nothing like passion and inspiration. After all, Martin Luther King said, "I have a dream," not, "I have a strategic plan."

Still, it's not enough to talk about saving the earth—we have to figure out what we're saving it from and what we're saving it for. The web of life, after all, *is* interconnected, and whether written by a screenwriter or spoken by a native chieftain in the nineteenth century it is largely true that what humans do to the web of life, they do to themselves. But ecological balance, like world peace, is an ever-elusive goal that is much harder to define, let alone achieve, than it is to dream about. We look at our growing children and crave the same kind of world for them that we craved for ourselves in the 1960s, but we are learning, learning, learning that the lessons are hard and the going is tough.

That's progress, I think. If we're less comfortable with what we see in the mirror than we were three decades ago, at least we're wrestling with the complexity of what it means to bring our society and our lifestyles into balance with the ability of the earth to sustain us. Our children—and grandchildren for a few—are no longer a metaphor, they're here with us and their presence has had a profound effect upon our outlook. This can only help.

We middle-aged veterans of the environmental movement should take increased devotion from the tremendous progress made by our movement to date and from the fact that we're really confronting the more nitty-gritty questions that remain. With malice toward none, save the few black hats still left over from the days when no one cared, we must persevere in a new way, with a new perspective that recognizes both the optimism of our youth and the pragmatism of our middle age.

(2004)

PART 2

Motives

The Mighty Yellowstone

Conquering Nature?

As I write and as you read this, small armies are preparing all over the world for assaults on nature. People are girding up for battles to be fought on all sorts of terrain from mountain to desert, in the air and on the water.

I refer not to military action of any sort, but to the analogy used by many people who climb mountains, run rivers, go backpacking, sail, or pursue other activities in the outdoors. For some reason, many people need to define their outdoor experience in terms of conflict.

We've all read the accounts: "How I Fought Mount Everest—and Won," or "Battling Against the Ocean," or numerous other tales of fights, battles, bouts, struggles, and other combat along the line of the "Humans Against Nature" theme. My response to these thrilling accounts of brutal conflict between human and the elements is to yawn and shake my head at how so many people could miss the obvious.

The mountain doesn't care if the climber makes it to the top or not. And it certainly doesn't "hurl" snowstorms at people, nor does it fling them off its slopes. As Hillary or Mallory or one of those intrepid adventurers observed, it's just there. The climber succeeds, fails, lives, or dies because of his or her decisions and skill, and perhaps a bit from chance. There's no malice on the mountain's part, nor is there any mercy. The mountain is detached from the climber. The sea doesn't rise up against a person's boat in anger, nor does it take particular note of it and try to smash it to bits. It's just there. Same with the desert, the jungle, or any other environment. The challenge is not in the mountain, the ocean, the trail, or the jungle. It is not in the charging elephant, the frightful storm, or the tricky winds. The challenge, in the end, is within ourselves.

I believe that one who climbs a mountain and believes that the mountain has somehow been defeated is deceiving himself. There is no defeat because there was nothing contested—the mountain didn't object to the climb; it just sat there. Though it might be a source of pride to think that one has "beaten" a mountain many thousands of feet high and quite massive and impressive in appearance, the fact is that we have mastered not the mountain but ourselves and our limitations. The sailor doesn't master the wind, he takes advantage of it—and the challenge is between the sailor himself and the boat. The water, wind, and waves are just there.

TO ME, IF ONE ESCAPES THE "MAN AGAINST NATURE" TRAP, THE EXPERIENCE of a challenging outdoor trip is not diminished, it is heightened. Mastery of the self is the ultimate challenge for each of us. To meet that challenge outdoors amid the spectacular scenery of a mountain range or the ocean or the desert is a wonderful experience. Nature is a great arena in which to challenge one's self. But to think you are challenging nature is to deceive yourself. It diminishes nature and it diminishes you.

There's a larger lesson here, too. If nature is simply the setting or context for a challenge to ourselves in adventurous outings, then it must also be simply the setting or context for our lives overall. The idea of competing with nature, though pervasive in our culture, is simply wrong. We would do well to adjust our thinking.

Rather than considering our relationship with nature as the establishment of some sort of truce between adversaries, let's recognize that nature isn't fighting us; we're fighting ourselves. We are fighting the agonizing battle of deciding among ourselves what sort of world we will have and how we will respond to the knowledge and skill we gain in dealing with the limitations nature, in quite impartial fashion, imposes on us. We are also fighting our tendency at times to overexploit and destroy.

Let's finally recognize that the activities we pursue which take a toll on natural resources represent not a victory in a nonexistent battle with nature, but the defeat of ourselves. The sooner we recognize that we don't beat mountains into submission when we climb them or tame rivers when we raft them, perhaps the sooner we can also start to understand that industrial development, discharge of chemicals into our surroundings, paving over of our landscape, and the destruction of wild places represent a struggle only within ourselves over what kind of world we will have. And let's not forget that, just as the mountain we climb doesn't care about us and will allow us to live or die based upon the choices we make when we climb, so our local and global environments will remain detached as we decide what our fate will be.

(Spring 1989)

Why Protect Land?

CONVENTIONAL WISDOM AND COMMON PORTRAYALS OF CONSERVATION IN THE media hold that the principal reason for saving wild country is that the many species it harbors might one day offer cures for cancer, remedies for arthritis, and other miracle cures. The potent anticancer drug Taxol, for example, comes from the Pacific yew, which environmentalists are striving to protect in the old-growth forests of the American West Coast.

There are certainly good reasons to believe that more research on the world's plants and animals will yield many drugs, cures, and remedies for a variety of diseases that plague humankind—after all, we are only now "discovering" herbal and natural remedies that were known to our ancestors and indigenous peoples for thousands of years. But there is another, more obvious therapeutic value to saving wild country: the tonic it provides for our souls.

I don't need to swallow a drug made from plant extracts in order to be soothed and healed by the wilderness. I don't need to see research studies and "proof" to know that wild country is good for humanity. I don't need a doctor to tell me that healing comes from wilderness; I've felt that for myself. I've lived it and breathed it and know it to be true with every fiber of my body.

Henry David Thoreau knew it when he "went to the woods to live deliberately." Walt Whitman knew it when he wrote that the secret of making the best persons is "to grow in the open air and to eat and sleep with the earth." Little children show it when their moods brighten and faces glow because they love to play outdoors. Suburbanites show it when they take the family dog for a walk in the park or watch birds at the backyard feeder. With little effort, one can find a thousand proofs that wild country is good for people.

We can also see the need for the materials and money produced by the progress that has accompanied humanity's beating back of the wilds. Modern medicine, science, and technology have helped to improve the human condition, too. But we can have too much of a good thing, can't we? Just as I wouldn't advocate that the entire world be returned to wilderness—we need cities, agriculture and places to live and work—I would argue that too much conquering of the wild is counterproductive. There's certainly nothing wrong with trying to make life easier for us than it was for our ancestors, but why do our efforts to overcome the adversity faced by our ancestors seem to lead us too far in the direction of creature comforts, conveniences, and just plain excess?

HUMAN BEINGS HAVE SHOWN THEMSELVES TO BE QUITE GOOD AT DEALING with adversity. In my estimation, this is because mechanisms to deal with problems are hardwired into our bodies and brains. We have a well-developed and well-documented flight/fight response, which supposedly developed from our ancestors' need to move quickly when physical danger threatened. We hear over and over that crises bring out the best in people, and we have documented that humans can instantly call up many effective ways for dealing with problems, adversity, and scarcity. It figures—our ancestors grew up in tough times and they didn't have the abundant food and the many modern conveniences available to us today.

But in using our brains and modern technology to overcome those problems, we have created for ourselves a world quite different from the one in which all those adaptations evolved. Physically adapted to the hunter-gatherer lifestyle of our ancestors, for example, our bodies store food so efficiently that a modern diet of abundant food has rendered most of our populace dangerously overweight. Avoiding excess was not a survival skill for our ancestors, but it has become one for us; we have discovered the need to self-regulate. And that is a very difficult challenge for us: though we come equipped with hardwired mechanisms for dealing with adversity and scarcity, when it comes to dealing with excess and abundance, we haven't an evolutionary clue.

Neither do we seem to have an effective antidote for the stress of our hectic lifestyle and the din of constant communications, extended now with cell phones to every corner of our lives. We're good at doing more, moving faster, and going farther, but we don't seem to easily recognize when we have reached the point of diminishing returns so that we can slow down and relax. Which brings us back to the topic of natural land: for the stresses and excesses of modern life, there's no better therapy than wild country.

People love wild country. Why else would so many flock to the Grand Canyon, Yellowstone, Yosemite, and other famous wild places? Why else would we have "white noise generators" and CDs that play the sound of rushing water, loon calls, and other natural sounds to wash away the stress induced by too many e-mails, express overnight documents, text messages, and cell phones that jolt one's midsection with a shock sensation even on "silent"? Does anyone prefer the warbling of a cellular phone to the whisper of wind in the pines?

WELL, YES, SAY SOME. THAT PHONE CALL MAY BRING IN THE BIG DEAL THAT will make me a pile of money and enable me to leave this rat race and build my place in the country and live happily ever after—provided I have a satellite link to check my investments every hour and . . . Uh-oh, what's wrong with this picture?

Which brings me to the little corner of northern Michigan where I live. We do a lot more sunset-watching and flower-sniffing around here, I'll wager, than people in many more populated places. I suspect that this is one reason why folks who can't make their year-round homes here will work hard nonetheless to escape to the North Country for a weekend (good), a long weekend (better), or a summer (heaven on earth!). Ditto for other resort destinations around the nation and around the world. The pace of life is saner, the opportunities to enjoy the outdoors more readily available, and that wild country we love is much closer at hand than it is in most people's hometowns.

But there's a danger: the rat race intrudes here, too. Cell phones, faxes, e-mail, and other modern contrivances that facilitate urgency are all around us. They press in on our North Country lifestyle, eroding the atmosphere of peace and tranquility, tempting us into dealing with life as if it were composed entirely of the challenges and adversities that activate the flight-or-fight response. It's very unhealthy, and tends to lead us back in the race with all the other rats. What to do?

Self-discipline is one answer, of course. Our consciousness and self-knowledge can help us meet the challenges that evolution has not equipped us to meet. The other, I think, is to keep wild country close at hand. For those of us who understand that Thoreau and Walt Whitman were on to something, it's a great victory every time someone "forgets" to bring the cell phone to watch a sunset or "accidentally" drops a pager into clear Great Lakes water while out on a boat. We're all a bit healthier, I think, if our daily commute takes us past a beautiful wild area where we are able to stop once in a while, walk in away from the noise of the roadway, and simply listen to the silence, smell the fresh forest-scented air, or take a walk along a pristine beach.

I AM CERTAINLY GLAD THAT THE PROTECTION OF WILD COUNTRY MAY ONE DAY lead to a cure for cancer, a better pain medicine, or perhaps even a remedy for my asthma. I agree that there are many benefits to be gained from further study of nature and her many hidden blessings. But when it comes to understanding the therapeutic value of nature and the importance of protecting wild land, those of us who live in or frequently visit the North Country don't need any new wonder drugs or miracle products to prove the point; we see it every day when we look through our windshields or out the back door. Natural land is in itself a form of therapy. It's good for us, it's important, and we need to keep it in all of our lives.

(Spring 1999)

The Biophilia Hypothesis

ONE OF THE THINGS THAT MOTIVATED ME TO CHOOSE A CAREER IN CONSER-vation was this solid belief that natural land is good for people. These feelings about the importance of nature to people have always been a sort of heartfelt or gut-level knowledge to many people as they are to me. But few of us could quote much scientific research to actually support the belief, even though the feeling remains strong and unshakable. As one writer put it, it's something you know deep inside, "with a certainty far more secure than intellect can offer."

Now, however, scientific work is demonstrating the importance of nature on the intellectual level as well as in the heart and gut. Edward O. Wilson, who is the Frank B. Baird, Jr. Professor of Science at Harvard University, has advanced what he terms the biophilia hypothesis. In Wilson's words, biophilia is "the innately emotional affiliation of human beings to other living organisms." Wilson believes biophilia to be "hereditary and hence part of ultimate human nature," and goes on to state that "the feelings . . . fall along several emotional spectra, from attraction to aversion, from awe to indifference, from peacefulness to fear-driven anxiety."

In a book edited by Wilson and Steven Kellert, who is professor of forestry and environmental studies at Yale, a number of researchers offer evidence that supports the biophilia hypothesis (*The Biophilia Hypothesis*, Island Press, edited by Stephen R. Kellert and Edward O. Wilson, 1993). Here, in scientific form, is a discussion of everything from our love of bluff-top views to our fear of spiders. The book establishes through research that there may indeed be something to the biophilia hypothesis and outlines its significance in relation to aesthetics, culture, symbolism, evolution, ethics, and political action.

THE IMPLICATIONS OF ALL THIS ARE BOTH FAR-REACHING AND PROFOUND. And, I would add for those of us who have long had a sort of gut feeling about the importance of nature to people, the evidence supporting the biophilia hypothesis represents a form of vindication. We're not just nature freaks trying to foist our agenda on others, after all; instead we are indeed in touch with something that is a very important part of humanity's heritage. As Kellert asserts in his introduction to the book, "The natural environment is critical to human meaning and fulfillment at both the individual and the societal level." Issues ranging from protecting the biodiversity of the earth's entire ecosystem to the need for parks in everyone's backyard take on a whole new meaning—and a whole new urgency.

I would guess that many people who love the outdoors will find little in Wilson and Kellert's book that is surprising. After all, we've recognized for a long time that nature is important to people. We've long believed that we're better off with nature close at hand, where we can spend time on beautiful shores, windswept dunes, majestic mountains, beautifully sculpted deserts, deep forests, or lovely, open meadows. We like to see the stars at night instead of the glare of sodium-vapor streetlamps, and we like the sound of the wind in the trees more than the sound of snarled traffic.

We're conservationists because we want to provide our children—and theirs, and theirs, and theirs—with the same opportunity we had: the opportunity to wander the woods, shores, and fields of an unspoiled land; to fish a quiet stream; to discover the variety of life outdoors and to become a part of nature, not just a spectator. Because land is the ultimate natural resource, we work to preserve natural land as the cradle from which everything in nature arose.

And we believe it important for everyone to have a share of the natural world available. Even though we're fortunate enough to have homes or cottages in the North Country—or in the mountains, the seashore, or some other naturally beautiful place—we must recognize that nature is equally important to those who currently do not have access to natural land. Those of us who have maintained that outdoor experience could be of great value to people in ridding our inner cities of problems may not be so far off base, after all. Consider this passage from Kellert's chapter on "The Biological Basis for Human Values of Nature":

> Nature's potential for providing a more satisfying existence may be less obvious and apparent among the poor and urban than the rich and rural, but this deprivation represents more of a challenge of design and opportunity than any fundamental irrelevance to the natural world for a class of people. . . . Society's obligation is not to bemoan the seeming 'absence' of nature in the inner city

or among the poor but to render its possibility more readily available. The presumption that only the materially advantaged and conveniently located can realize nature's value represents an arrogant characterization.

Kellert and Wilson's book has enough footnotes and scientific terminology to separate it from works like Aldo Leopold's *Sand County Almanac* or the writings of Thoreau. Still, its importance to the conservation movement and to humanity in general should not be underestimated. Though the biophilia hypothesis is still just an emerging theory, the signs are clear that we are about to witness a historic convergence of science and spirit as it becomes more widely accepted that the need to identify with nature is indeed an innate part of each and every human being.

"The Biophilia Hypothesis" represents a wake-up call for those who have doubted the importance of keeping nature close at hand for all humanity. It is a challenge to those who would shrug off the preservation of natural land and biodiversity as the special interest of a privileged elite. For those of us who are involved in the conservation cause, it is a call to take time out for a moment of celebration, and then get back to work.

(Summer 1994)

Science and Spirit

IT IS ALL WELL AND GOOD TO UNDERSTAND THAT SCIENCE IS NOW CONFIRMING that natural land is good for people. However, I believe it important to resist the common Western temptation to view science as being somehow superior to spirit when it comes to the importance of natural land.

THE PRESERVATION OF TROPICAL RAIN FORESTS AND OTHER NATURAL LAND, for example, is often portrayed by the media and by environmental groups themselves as vital to the survival of the human species for reasons relating to science and scientifically documented importance. The biodiversity argument is the principal example: humans' continued presence on the earth, we are told, cannot be assured unless we promote biodiversity, reserve a certain amount of forested land for producing oxygen, and so on. We must save this, that, or the other parcel of land, we are admonished, because in so doing we will save some species of herb or bug that science will use to one day cure everything from cancer to Aunt Millie's lumbago. It's the same familiar refrain.

But, while agreeing that we must by all means take a careful, scientific look at land preservation, I see the scientific calculus of survival as representing only one aspect of a much larger and even more challenging issue. Saving land to save our species is a noble goal, but I think that by hanging our collective hats too firmly on the biodiversity issue, we give short shrift to the importance of saving natural land for its value to the human soul and spirit, not to mention the importance of maintaining the spirit of the land itself. To maintain a close connection with the land, I maintain, is much more than to ensure the survival of medicinal plants and such; it is to prevent the impoverishment of the human spirit and the loss of perspective on our place as an integral part of nature. Along with survival as a species, we must assure survival of the human spirit, for the decline of the human soul and spirit is also a key threat to our species.

This is not to say that science is unnecessary; to the contrary, I believe it has tremendous importance. But the nature of that importance to conservation is overblown, I think, if we see the environment as only a science issue and miss out on the equally, if not more, important aesthetic and spiritual side.

The spiritual side is what Thoreau had in mind when he went to the woods to live and declared that "in wildness is the preservation of the world." The spiritual side is what we call to mind when we speak of the American Pioneer Spirit and of the rugged men and tireless women who made lives for themselves living close to the land on the American frontier, developing in themselves and their children a strength of character and spirit which helped to make our nation and our people great. The spiritual side is what Aldo Leopold had in mind when he made his famous declaration, "I am glad that I shall never be young without wild country to be young in." The spiritual side of natural land is what moves you when you see a beautiful sunset, takes your breath away when looking over a vast, wild landscape, or captures your sense of mystery as you look into the heavens on a starry night.

UNFORTUNATELY, SEEING THE SPIRITUAL IMPORTANCE OF THINGS SEEMS always to be tough for those of us who grew up in Western cultures. Steeped as we are in the supposedly concrete world of Aristotle, Newton, and linear, oppositional thinking, we gravitate toward that which we can quantify, define, and dissect. We cannot seem to equal those from Eastern or Western indigenous cultures in their ability to deal with paradox or with the circular, cyclic, and mystical. Maybe that's why we seem to relate more easily to terms like "biodiversity" and prospects for medical breakthroughs than we do to concepts like "beauty," "wildness," and the prospects for human enrichment that come with spending time outdoors. We seem to deal more easily with the facts of nature, like numbers and names, than we do with the feel of nature, which has to do with the sound of a loon in the wild, the beauty of a sun-dappled forest floor, or the mystery and wonder of shimmering northern lights on a North Woods winter's eve.

In fact, there seem to be two types of conservationists: the scientific and the spiritual. Scientific conservationists tend to quantify, dissect, and analyze nature, while spiritual conservationists identify more closely with the experience of the outdoors, the feeling of natural systems and the spirit of the land. When it comes to setting priorities for conservation, the "scientific school" holds that we must categorize and quantify and preserve this and that species or habitat for reasons of supposedly objective science. Meanwhile, the more spiritually oriented among our ranks tend toward the belief that if we protect and care for enough wild country to fulfill the human need to enjoy nature in its unfettered splendor and to give our own existence a proper sense of context, we will in so doing automatically manage to include enough of this or that habitat for a full complement of species to accompany us into the future. Biodiversity seems to represent the goal of the scientific school, while it is the by-product of the spiritual. The two approaches seem hopelessly at odds. Or are they?

I recall an interesting example offered at a staff training workshop that focused on the different ways that people experience the world, communicate, and behave. While several distinctly different styles were explained, it was emphasized that none is necessarily "better" than another; it is simply a matter of the preferences or tendencies we have, like the preference each of us tends to exhibit for using the right or left hand in most activities. We have and need two hands, but as right- or left-handed people, we simply show a preference for one or the other.

So IT IS, I THINK, WITH THE SCIENCE AND SPIRIT OF CONSERVATION. ONE'S approach to conservation from the perspective of science or spirit is like the tendency to use the right or left hand. Perhaps we are born with this preference, or perhaps we learn it; in any event, the preference is there. But where there is preference, there are alternatives from which to choose. And where there are alternatives, there can be balance, conciliation, and even unity.

In reading the works of scientists like Einstein and Bohm, or the words of sages like Krishnamurti or the Dalai Lama, it becomes clear that the same sense of mystery and wonder at the nature of our world comes to both the scientist and the sage. The scientific and the spiritual, we find, are not so much opposite and distant from one another on a linear scale as they are complementary and necessary to one another on different sides of a circle. Views that seemed to oppose and exclude one another turn out to be, in fact, necessary to one another and in the end directly connected.

So, even though conservation is so often portrayed as primarily an affair of science, fear not if you have an interest in conservation but not much knowledge or love of science. It is just as important to care for the beauty and symmetry of nature as it is to know about biodiversity. It is as important to provide our children with a beautiful earth to inherit as it is a sustainable one; in fact, the two are ultimately the same. It is as important, if not more so, to care about the whole of the earth as it is to dissect and understand its parts. The job of taking care of our earth and our corner of it can be approached with the right or left hand—the scientific or the spiritual. Neither is superior to the other, neither is "better," except to the extent that it suits each person to take his or her own approach.

I believe in the importance of spirit in conservation along with the importance of science. I believe that the conservation movement and our society would be better off if we could all afford greater recognition to the fact that the earth belongs to scientist and sage alike, and that proper stewardship of that precious earth is a matter of both science and spirit.

(Summer 1993)

Dark Sky Park

WHAT IF I TOLD YOU THAT, WHEREVER YOU LIVE, YOU ARE AT MOST WITHIN A few minutes' drive of being able to peer into one of the most vast and beautiful wilderness areas people have ever seen? What if I told you that this great wild place has had only a few dozen human visitors in all of recorded history, and that it appears the same before our eyes today as it did to our ancestors hundreds and even thousands of years ago? And what if I also told you that this is the very same wilderness that has inspired and illustrated the myths and legends of virtually every culture the world has ever known?

Would you be inclined to take a few minutes and have a look for yourself? Would you say that it is important for all of us to protect the view of this wonderful place so that future generations can experience the same sense of awe and wonder that inspired our ancestors and can still inspire us all today? Are you curious about exactly where this beautiful, wonder-filled place can be found? If you answered yes to any of those questions, welcome to the ranks of people who are taking a new look at an old familiar friend: the night sky.

It's all there, free for the viewing: constellations, vast spaces, beautiful lights, twinkling colors and endless wonder. The steadiness of the stars in their places, the slow wandering of the planets through the heavens. The occasional visits of comets and the breathtaking spectacle of shooting stars. Moonrise and moonset, the ethereal dance of the northern lights, and the mystical glow of things like noctiluminescent clouds. Galaxies, nebulae, and other worlds. Up There, we can see all of the Great Dramas that have played out in our history and mythology: from the Greek and Roman myths many of us studied in school to the Norse legends, African tales, and American Indian stories that address the Big Questions about who we are and why we're here. No admission charged and no telescope required.

The Little Traverse Conservancy has a special connection to night sky viewing through Emmet County's Headlands park, acquired with assistance from the Conservancy, which holds a conservation easement on the land. The Headlands has been designated as the sixth International Dark Sky Park in the United States, and the ninth in the world. In part a tribute to the work of the late Gary Williams, who served a number of years on the Conservancy's board of trustees, the Dark Sky Park also owes its gratitude to Mary Stewart Adams. For the past decade, Mary has championed the cause of what one might call "dark sky conservation" in the North and now serves as program director for the Headlands on behalf of Emmet County.

A key feature of the International Dark Sky Park is control of stray light, or "light pollution" from surrounding areas. Many northern Michigan communities, businesses, and residents are discovering that traditional outdoor lighting often casts so much glare that one can barely see the stars at night. But there are relatively easy fixes for this that provide adequate illumination while not interfering with the beauty of the night sky.

Conservancy trustee Dave Kring won an award from the regional Outdoor Lighting Forum for the excellent job done on lighting for his auto dealership that illuminates the building and cars without obliterating the view of the moon, stars, and planets whirling overhead. The town of Elk Rapids won a similar award after it refitted its street lighting to protect the night sky view, and as this issue goes to press the Village of Mackinaw City is embarking on a similar project. Importantly, these lighting improvement projects also produced significant energy (and operating cost) savings as a bonus.

What a wonderful thing this is! Just as the Conservancy works to keep the beauty of natural land close at hand, thanks to Gary's vision and Mary's inspiration and leadership, the people of our area are working together to keep the glorious beauty of the night sky close at hand as well.

Part of the beauty of the night sky is that it represents so many things to us. The fictional Captain Kirk of the starship *Enterprise* famously declared it "the final frontier," and the sky can inspire us as can remnants of the American frontier in places like our great national parks. In the Space Age, we can look directly at space itself—and the wonders that occupy it. We can contemplate vast distances, scientific theories, and technological wonders. It's all connected in our heritage. The ancient art of astrology, we must remember, was the forerunner of what became the science of astronomy. It was the starry sky that most inspired our ancestors when they contemplated their place on the earth and in Creation. These same stars have been dreamed of, sung about, worshiped, sought after, and wished upon throughout the entire existence of humankind. To protect the night sky is to have not only a vast wilderness area but also a museum of science, mythology, and human culture before us every cloudless night.

As Mary so eloquently says, it doesn't matter whether your attention to the starry skies is focused through a telescope or a horoscope. We are all linked to the night sky, and the night sky is an important part of what links us to one another.

In the age of computers, smart phones, HDTV, and an expression called "screen time" to define the hours we spend before electronic devices, it's good to know that people are working to protect the view of the night sky so that it is possible to head outside, look up, and experience the primal wonder of the vastness of the heavens. No telescope required. No electrical outlet or device.

Just one's eyes, and perhaps some companions to revel in the beauty and wonder of the Ultimate Wilderness: the night sky above us.

(Fall 2011)

Locking Up Land

OVER THE THIRTY-PLUS YEARS I HAVE BEEN INVOLVED IN EFFORTS TO PRO-tect wilderness and natural areas, I have heard voices in opposition accusing wilderness protection advocates of trying to "lock up" natural resources.

It's a familiar line. "You just want to lock this land away," they howl, "and keep people from using the minerals and timber and then converting the land to use for houses, roads, and businesses." This pronouncement is frequently accompanied by sermons about letting resources go to waste and about the tragedy of ruling out "productive use." We conservation advocates are told that we're selfish and that a good capitalist wouldn't lock away those valuable resources.

Rubbish. A good capitalist *does* save resources. You don't spend your capital, you protect it and make it grow. Savings aren't lost; they're saved, quite literally, for the future. People save their money and companies save their resources. Money and resources saved are available in case of need. It's prudent to save, and it makes good common sense. It isn't selfish, either, if it helps to provide future citizens, owners, or stockholders with more prosperity and more options.

If saving resources for the future and making them available for the use of our children and theirs is "locking them up," then so be it. It makes good economic sense as well as good resource management sense. We should not burn the last drop of oil, nor cut the last old-growth tree, nor hoard for ourselves the natural wealth that should rightfully be managed for the benefit of our children. We should not limit the biological diversity of the earth for our own shortsighted interests when it is entirely possible that our grandchildren may have both scientific and aesthetic needs for species that were recklessly destroyed by their shortsighted forebears.

I look at the lockup issue from another viewpoint: I believe that development locks up land and resources in a far more irretrievable fashion than does preservation and protection. Development takes the land and resources out of savings, committing them to intensive use. I've seen thousands of natural areas taken in my lifetime to build houses, roads, shopping malls, apartments, offices, and mines and for other uses. I've seen ponds and swamps and lakes drained and destroyed, forever lost. I've seen houses torn down to develop businesses, businesses torn down to develop factories, and just about everything torn down to develop highways and shopping malls. But *never* have I seen a housing development, a shopping mall, a highway, or an office building turned back into a natural area.

PROTECTED NATURAL LAND, ON THE OTHER HAND, CAN BE TAKEN OUT OF SAVings if ever the need should arise. If our society becomes desperate for resources, Congress could sell the national parks, opening Yellowstone to timber, mining, and grazing interests. We could, if we decide that land protection is a luxury we can no longer afford, outlaw conservation easements and allow the haphazard development of every square inch of the North Country. Those decisions will be made by our children, and that is as it should be; it will be their world, after all.

But I don't worry that those things will ever come to pass. I believe, instead, that as those natural areas and resources are appreciated by generation after generation, they will be valued more and more. Like our great national parks, the natural areas we are setting aside today will become increasingly precious to our children, and theirs and theirs.

We have the right and the responsibility to protect a share of our land from development and exploitation. It has become a cliché to say that land is not inherited from our parents but borrowed from our children. Nonetheless, we must provide our children with natural areas to enjoy and decisions to make about what they will do with the land. If we have committed it all to exploitation and development, we have deprived our successors of the right to choose what sort of world they will live in. That would truly lock away many alternatives.

We need to teach our children about the importance of saving money, land, and resources, and that saving natural land makes as much sense as protecting one's economic capital. We need to leave our children a world that has not been stripped of everything with value for the gratification of their selfish and shortsighted parents. We need to teach the lesson that the decision to destroy a natural area and develop it is a decision that cannot be reversed, because once land is altered by human activity, its natural value is indeed locked away forever.

(Winter 1990)

PART 3

Hunting

Woods at Cross Village

The Hunting Issue: Some Background

AMPLE EVIDENCE SHOWS THAT AT THE DAWN OF HUMAN CULTURE, PEOPLE were drawn together by common interests and goals that revolved around basic survival. Survival—procurement of food, water, and shelter for basic subsistence—required everyone's time, energy, and effort. Groups, it turned out, had better prospects for survival than isolated individuals, and so human communities were born. As human society developed and people became more adept and efficient at meeting their basic needs, they began to have time and energy for interests that extended beyond mere survival. As humans have developed the technological ability to vastly extend the range of human activity, it has made possible an ever-increasing diversity of human endeavors and ways of looking at the world.

Hunting and hunter-gatherer cultures were the norm for most of human existence. But the advent of agriculture some 10,000 years ago, then mass agriculture in the last few centuries began to change that. This change has accelerated now that our technological society has made it quite possible for people to live without any direct association with hunting and gathering. For the first time in human history, one can live and eat quite comfortably without having the slightest firsthand knowledge of where the food comes from.

Similarly, hunting and agriculture have come to be viewed and used by many people not as mechanisms for basic survival but as leisure activities. Recreational gardening and sport hunting are two examples. The roles of domestic animals have changed, too, evolving from necessity to leisure. Not needed so much for work and food, animals have become pets, pastimes, and status symbols.

The evolution of hunting, agriculture, and human society obviously took place over a very long period of time. By contrast, the history of what we know as the conservation movement has been fairly brief, corresponding to the explosive growth over the last couple of centuries of human-driven technology and the explosive growth of human population.

The conservation movement in American society first came to the fore with the likes of Theodore Roosevelt, Gifford Pinchot, and John Muir. The dedication of Yellowstone as the world's first national park in 1872 was a significant event, as was development of the U.S. National Forest system and many other developments as the nineteenth century gave way to the twentieth. A prime focus of this early conservation movement was not only to keep some areas of our country untouched for all to enjoy, but also to assure a continuing supply of game, timber, and minerals to support a growing nation.

The second wave of the conservation movement corresponded to the well-known programs of the Great Depression. The Great Dust Bowl gave rise to new developments in soil conservation, and programs like the Civilian Conservation Corps undertook a vast number and variety of conservation projects aimed, again, at helping to ensure the continuing availability of resources. The focus expanded somewhat during this second wave, from forests and game to include recreation, watershed values, and protection from forest and prairie fires. Writers and scholars like Aldo Leopold not only wrote their now-famous works celebrating the beauty and joy of the outdoors (such as Leopold's immortal *A Sand County Almanac*) but also advanced the environmental sciences through such works as Leopold's very influential but much less well known *Game Management*. The hunting question was important during this second wave, and Leopold himself mused in his writings about how it can be possible to love ducks and shoot them, too.

As the second wave of conservation awareness began to ebb, Rachel Carson's *Silent Spring* provided the cornerstone for the third wave, which would become known in the 1970s as the environmental movement. By the time this movement developed, most Americans were urban residents, not rural folk, and the focus of the movement had shifted away from providing continuing supplies of timber and game to embrace global concerns about human population, environmental pollution, and the issue of human activity modifying not only the climate but the entire global balance of life on earth. Human society was vastly more complex than it had been during the previous two conservation movements, and most people's livelihoods were farther removed from direct association with the land than at any time in previous human history. Hunting and gathering were not primary issues anymore. Because of progress made in the previous two movements, populations of many of the more commonly hunted game species had stabilized or improved: bison were back from the brink of extinction, pronghorn antelope had made a comeback, and market hunting was largely a thing of the past. The lessons learned from such sad episodes as the extinction of the passenger pigeon had been applied with great success to overall game management, thanks in no small measure to the contributions of people like Aldo Leopold in the previous wave of conservation concern.

THE ANIMAL RIGHTS MOVEMENT BEGAN TO TAKE HOLD DURING THE THIRD wave of conservation, made possible by a culture that had come to see hunting not as a necessity but as a leisure activity, luxury, or even an anachronism. Most people's exposure to animals was not to wild creatures or farm stock but to pets, to media portrayals of a wildly exaggerated and idealized life in the wild, or to exhibitions in zoos.

This was in contrast to the views of hunters and anglers, who had been the leaders in the earlier conservation movements. The efforts of hunters and anglers had provided momentum for the earlier conservation movement through self-imposed taxes on guns, ammunition, and fishing equipment along with license fees for hunting and fishing. Hunters and anglers were justifiably proud that billions of dollars had been poured into conservation programs as a result of the efforts of hunters and anglers to tax themselves and limit their activities for the good of the resource. But suddenly, as the environmental movement blossomed in the 1970s, the traditional conservation constituency of hunters and anglers was confronted by people who identified themselves as conservationists or environmentalists but who held a radically different view of the relationship between people and animals. These new activists held that hunters and anglers were the enemy.

A split thus evolved between those conservation interests that hold hunting and fishing to be important and legitimate human activities versus those who contend that hunting and angling are primitive, barbaric, or environmentally unsound and should be severely limited or done away with. Led by TV and movie stars who often had little or no direct experience with hunting and fishing, animal rights fervor grew in the 1970s and 1980s as people conveniently omitted Leopold's contention that one could love ducks and shoot them too in favor of using his other passages to justify an end to hunting and fishing. Trapping and the fur industry, especially, took the brunt of the opposition.

And so there continues to be a major split within the conservation or environmental cause between those who support continued hunting and fishing and those who oppose these activities. The division and infighting created by this split has significantly reduced the movement's ability to promote its agenda both publicly and politically, and though both groups have much in common, the battle lines seem to be becoming more firmly drawn and the sides are digging in for a protracted struggle.

As an original Earth Day activist who clearly sees the need for pollution control, and at the same time as one who has supported conservation through hunting and fishing license fees and special taxes on shooting and fishing equipment, I see both sides' concerns and only lament the detrimental effect the split has had on our movement overall. The stereotypes, admittedly oversimplified here and used only for example, are these: The Hunter, who has been paying self-imposed taxes on sporting equipment and licenses for years, claims superiority because he or she has been paying directly for conservation over all this time. He or she obeys game laws, carefully works to protect the lands and waters that provide natural benefits, and objects strenuously to a bunch of Johnnie-come-latelies to the movement who scream about animal rights, demand free access to land purchased with hunters' and anglers' dollars, and propose to kick the hunter and angler out because of some superior moral claim to what's best for the environment.

The Hunter argues that hunting has been part of human culture as long as there has been human culture; to deny this or to say that humans are not adapted to be hunters is to deny nature, not to embrace it. The idea that humans must keep hands off animals promotes the view of humanity as separate from nature, not part of it, and this is simply wrong. In terms of animal "rights," if we humans are indeed but one of the animal species who share the earth, don't humans have as much right to be predators as other animals? As long as we use our consciousness and intelligence to ensure that we do not deplete the supplies of game or habitat, hunting is and should be a proper part of human culture.

The Animal Advocate, on the other hand, sees things as evolving differently. Primitive humans who had to kill animals for food evolved a system of gathering and agriculture that made the human role of predator obsolete. We now have it within our power to live well without killing animals, especially for sport, and we have a sacred moral and ethical obligation to stop inflicting harm on our fellow beings. Humans must strive for enlightenment, and enlightened behavior does not involve the pointless torturing and killing of fellow beings. Humans are no different from other animals, after all, and just as it is morally unjustifiable to kill another human without reason, so it is not justifiable to kill another animal for no reason. Enjoyment of the hunt or kill does not justify such action.

It seems as though it could go on forever. Both advocacy groups cling to their ends of what many tend to see as a linear spectrum, with hunting at one end and animal rights on the other.

I WOULD ARGUE THAT THE RIFT BETWEEN HUNTERS AND ANTIHUNTERS IS AS much a product of this linear thought process as it is a product of particular views about animals, humans, and hunting. We who have been steeped in Western culture tend to see things in linear fashion, and we take a reductionist view that everything can be broken down to its basic building blocks, analyzed, and completely explained in black-and-white terms. But maybe it's not so simple. Maybe linear thinking isn't the answer here, and perhaps we need to find new ways of looking at the issue. Perhaps the way to that new view can be illuminated by starting with the ultimate perspective—nature's.

(March 2000)

Nature-Based People's Perspective on Hunting

ONE OF THE MOST MEANINGFUL CONVERSATIONS I HAVE HAD ABOUT HUNTING was shared with a friend a few years ago. The talk took place in the context of a trip to consult with the owners of a large parcel of land in the Rocky Mountains that included some important winter elk habitat. The land was being severely overgrazed by mule deer, and some people advocated reduction of the mule deer population through hunting. Others, opposed to hunting for a number of reasons, objected.

I had recently read a book about shamanism, which has been an extremely important feature in human culture. American Indians, Australian Aborigines, African tribal people, South Americans, Asians, Pacific cultures, and, yes, even the tribal ancestors of Europeans have cultural roots in shamanism. Many shamanistic cultures are referred to as "nature based," an appropriate reference to their closeness to the natural world. Among other things, shamanism often involves the idea that people exhibit attributes of a particular animal whose spirit is close to them. A strong person may be said to be like the bison; a swift runner like the rabbit, cheetah, or deer; a good hunter like the wolf or lion. Animal spirits are called upon to guard and guide the individuals who are most closely associated with that particular spirit. For some reason, I began to think of the hunting debate in terms of how it might be viewed in a traditional or shamanistic culture. Hunters would be viewed as wolf people, lion people, hawk people, and so on. Those who favor a vegetarian lifestyle might be considered deer, buffalo, or rabbit people. Those in the middle might be associated with omnivorous animals, like the bear who eats plants and meat, or the fox, coyote, or a number of other omnivores.

HOW WOULD IT CHANGE OUR VIEW OF THE HUNTING DEBATE IF WE TRIED, for a time, to see things as they might appear in shamanistic culture? Certainly we would have to afford people their views in accordance with their respective animal spirits. No one can blame wolf for being wolf: therefore, we would need to respect wolf's need to hunt and the role wolf plays in the web of life. Likewise, we would have to acknowledge that deer does not need to eat meat, and therefore should not be expected to think or feel like wolf. We would also need to recognize that many of us fall in the middle somewhere; like fox, coyote, and bear we are more opportunistic and have more varied tastes. We would even need to make room for the gluttonous blue jay, the jackal, and others with which many of us might not want to identify when we view them in human terms, but which have their place in nature. All need to eat, somehow, and all have their places on Mother Earth, who loves and cares for all of her own.

To cite a parallel example involving the gathering side of our hunter-gatherer origins, I've read that some anthropologists and psychology researchers believe that many people's infatuation with shopping might actually be a throwback to our hunter-gatherer roots. Modern people are so cut off from the natural world, the theory goes, that our natural drive to find food now finds its expression in the compulsion to shop—the compulsion to find and gather things that we can use for food, for clothing, and for our homes. Compulsive shopping is simply the human gathering urge trying to find meaningful expression in a world that has failed to provide adequate opportunities for its most appropriate exercise. Could it be that the hunting debate is a manifestation of the same sort of thing—except that it involves the question of how modern humans with an inborn urge to hunt can fulfill their need to pursue game?

Some have argued that human consciousness gives us the ability to "rise above" our animal natures and become something more. But which nature is it that we should aspire to rise above? Is the higher expression of our humanity to be found in rising to the level of the hunter or rising to the level of the herbivore? Different cultures offer different answers. Who is to say which is more "enlightened"?

If we expand from a shamanistic to an ecological view of life, we can see that the earth makes room and has need for all of the various natures. Hunters, grazers, browsers, scavengers, and opportunistic omnivores all have their rightful place on the earth. Deer must be deer, wolf must be wolf. Bear must be bear and human must be human. Among humans, perhaps there is simply more diversity than among, say, hawks. Whether we believe in shamanism or not, perhaps there will always be elk people and lion people—herbivores and carnivores—and perhaps each should be forgiven for not quite understanding the other. If our fundamental natures prevent us from completely understanding one another, perhaps our consciousness can enable us to transcend those differences, understanding the need for acceptance. Perhaps consciousness is the key to understanding our ultimate need for one another.

THINKING IN SHAMANISTIC TERMS MAY NOT IMMEDIATELY RESOLVE THE debate about hunting issues. But perhaps it can expand our thinking just enough to open the path to a new dialogue that recognizes the legitimacy of both hunters and nonhunters among human beings. Perhaps if we think in shamanistic and ecological terms we can begin to understand that we need all strands in the web of life, no matter how distasteful the ways of one may seem to another. It will do us little good to argue over whether the higher moral position is occupied by the fruit eater, the plant eater, or the meat eater. All are linked together in a profound and beautiful system that, despite all our science and all our supposed knowledge, we are barely beginning to understand.

Seeing one another through the eyes of a shamanistic culture will be viewed by some as "primitive." But the shamanistic view may be more advanced than we think. A look back into human culture shows that humanity is merely a reflection of the great web of life in all its beauty, complexity, and diversity. Of course there are differences. Of course there are herbivores, carnivores, and omnivores—they're all linked together just as *we* are all linked together. The earth, I think, is showing us that we need one another, whether we choose to understand that or not.

(Fall 1996)

But Is There Room for Hunters?

THE GRAY WOLF, PROBABLY ONE OF THE FINEST EXAMPLES IN NORTH AMERICA of a skilled and effective wild hunter, is only beginning to be seen by European settlers and their descendants in our country as something other than a "bad" animal to be pursued, hated, and eliminated. Other predators such as coyotes, hawks, owls, eagles, grizzly bears, foxes, and more have been persecuted like the wolf because they are hunters. Even killer whales were portrayed as wanton assassins of the sea until it was discovered that they are more intelligent than first thought and that they can survive for a time in captivity, during which they will put on a show for us humans. Civilization, it seems, does not generally think highly of predation.

And so today, conservationists are working feverishly to restore the tarnished image of wolves and other predators. Avian predators in particular, such as hawks and owls, are being promoted as "not as bad as we once thought" in a variety of PR campaigns. It is particularly interesting that some of the principal advocates of taking a more humane and merciful view of predators tend to come from the animal rights or antihunting elements of the conservation and environmental movements.

Thus it is even more intriguing that while animal predators have had a tough time gaining acceptance in our culture, predators of the human variety have had the same trouble. One of the most insightful perspectives on this situation was articulated by retired Michigan wildlife biologist Jack Cook in his "Conservation Reflections" column in the *North Woods Call*. Jack, a colleague of my father's and family friend throughout my life, wrote about his readings of James Fennimore Cooper's *Leatherstocking Tales* and his interpretation of the character Natty Bumppo as a sort of symbol of the hunter, forced to retreat before the advance of civilization. "The free wandering world is destroyed by civilized society," Jack wrote. "As our country became civilized and regulated by manmade law, the freewheeling hunters and trappers were no longer needed."

Indeed, there are even more examples of "civilized" society rejecting the hunter. American Indians, largely a free-roaming people who hunted, gathered, and grew a few crops for their subsistence, were squeezed out by a growing American society that felt compelled to reduce land to the status of property and to drastically curtail the ability of animals to roam and of humans to hunt them. In fact, when it became "necessary" to do so, society resorted to eliminating the prey in order to eliminate the hunter, nearly driving the buffalo to extinction in this crazed quest. Hunters—both Indian and white alike—were forced farther out beyond the frontier, out to places where there was no pressure to adopt "civilized" ways and, ironically enough, to where they could blaze the trail for still more westward expansion that would eventually bring about the end of the frontier and the beginning of the end of the hunting life.

Could it be that the "need" to eliminate Indians from standing in the way of agriculture, railroads, and white settlement is only partly a study in racism, and is actually partly a study in civilization's apparent inability to coexist with the hunter? The mountain men and other hunters were forced away westward along with the Indians, until there was no room left for them and the frontier hunter was extinct. Witness Daniel Boone's continual quest for "elbow room."

That civilization has this inability to embrace, accept, or even tolerate the hunter is clear. Sure, in European society, a certain amount of hunting is carried on as a sport of kings and nobles, but the hunting lifestyle as a means of subsistence has been gone from Europe for centuries—since the days when the sheriff of Nottingham supposedly pursued Robin Hood for the unpardonable crime of killing the king's deer for himself, his band, and the peasants.

ALL THIS TROUBLES ME. IN REJECTING BOTH THE HUMAN HUNTER AND THE animal predator, I fear that we are rejecting something in ourselves that we should embrace and examine rather than sweep under the rug. Like it or not, human beings are omnivorous—part hunters—as any zoologist can tell us. Hunting is part of our history and genetic makeup, a factor in our adaptation over the centuries, and, as a number of researchers would no doubt affirm, hunting is imprinted deeply in the cortex of our brains. Why is it that we seem, as a group, so anxious to disclaim and reject the hunters among us and the hunting part of ourselves?

Jack Cook sees implications for the debate over hunting and trapping today. Seeing the increase in pressure to limit or eliminate hunting and trapping, he asks, "To what place can the modern day hunter and trapper go?" The frontier is gone and the Indian reservations are not able to contain all tribal members. The New England partridge hunter has fewer and fewer places to go, and in all parts of the country, people assert that animals have the right to not be hunted, even as many of these animals themselves are hunters.

Perhaps Jack Cook is right, and civilization is simply incompatible with the hunting life. Though we may manage to keep a remnant population around, there will never really be room for the wolf again. The Indian hunter, the mountain man, and even the weekend grouse hunter will just have to find other ways to get along. Perhaps our society will assert that animals have some right to escape from the claws, jaws, or guns of hunters. Perhaps.

Or perhaps we can recognize that if we are to preserve the natural world and to preserve humanity, then we must also make room to preserve both the animal and the human hunter. Perhaps we will find ways for people to accept hunting not as a threat or some savage sickness, but as something that is a part of each and every one of us whether we choose to express and admit it or not. Perhaps we can understand that the call of the loon and the wolf—both hunters—are seen as symbols of the wild because there can only be wild places if there are also hunters. Perhaps we'll recognize that while we cannot all be mountain men, we can save enough room and enough resources to enable significant numbers of us, who so choose, to continue to hunt as humans have since those dark, dim years so many millennia ago when mammals arose from the ashes of the dinosaurs.

THERE WILL BE NO MORE PEOPLE LIKE NATTY BUMPPO. THE AMERICAN Indians have little hope of living the life their great-great-grandparents lived, and gray wolves will no longer roam as much of the American continent as they once did. As Aldo Leopold observed, "Man always kills the things he loves and so we the pioneers have killed our wilderness." But as Leopold also observed, "Be that as it may, I am glad I shall never be young without wild country to be young in. Of what avail are forty freedoms without a blank spot on the map?" Today, we can still hear the cry of the wolf and the song of the loon and can still know hunters or even choose to hunt ourselves. Will we be able to say the same for our grandchildren?

(Winter 1993)

A Glimpse of How It Might Be . . .

THE DOG WAS ON POINT. ITS GRAY-HAIRED OWNER KNEW THAT THE BIRD WAS probably a grouse and that it probably wouldn't stay put for long. "Move up quick, right behind the dog," he said to the boy. "Get ready to shoot."

The boy moved quickly, tense with excitement, all senses on full alert. He nervously felt again for the safety on the 20-gauge shotgun, ready to flick it off but, as his grandfather had taught him, not until the moment came to shoot. His eyes swept beyond the dog ahead of him as he quickly forced his way through the tangled dry bracken ferns and densely packed pole-sized aspen trees.

Ready as he was, the flush of the bird caught him completely by surprise. (They always do, his grandfather had told him on a number of occasions, most notably a half-hour earlier when the boy missed shots at two flushing birds.) It sounded like thunder as the bird erupted from the cover, heading out and away at what seemed like the speed of light. But the boy's reactions were quick. Though the raising of the gun, release of the safety, and alignment of barrel and eye were not the automatic motions they are for more seasoned hunters, the boy's quickness made up for what he lacked in conditioning: the gun came up, the safety came off, and he slapped the trigger. For the first time, he didn't feel the kick of the gun; the bird fell in a shower of feathers. His first kill.

"Dead bird, Jennie," the owner shouted to the dog. "Fetch." Then, to the boy, "Good shooting, kiddo, good shooting!" The boy smiled nervously, the smell of powder filling his nostrils and a sense of both surprise and accomplishment sweeping over him. The grandfather strode forward, removing the shells from his own gun to a coat pocket. He extended his hand to his grandson, beaming. "You're a hunter now," he said.

THE DOG RETURNED WITH THE BIRD, OFFERING IT TO HER MASTER AND THEN busied herself with sniffing about where the scent was already fading. The boy looked at the bird, like dozens of others he'd seen his grandfather take over the years from the autumn woods. But it was different now. He had just killed this bird, and his initial elation at making his first successful kill was dampened as the warm, limp body of the grouse lay in his hand. Just a moment ago, this bird had been alive and conscious and thundering through the aspens, but now it would fly no more. He'd killed it, and was surprised that he didn't feel happier, given his determination just a few minutes ago to prove that he could hit live birds with the little shotgun he had used to break so many clay targets in practice.

His grandfather knew all too well what the boy was feeling. But he had some feelings of his own—strong, deep feelings about the hunting tradition, about life and about learning one's way in the outdoors. It was uncharacteristic of him to show his feelings too much, but here beneath the aspens something came over him. "Sit down for a minute, boy," the grandfather said, as he himself stood tall. "My grandson is a hunter now," he began. "My grandson has made his first kill after practicing and learning and waiting and watching for years. My grandson is a hunter."

He looked skyward. "I am a small, old, and weak man, but I ask you to hear me now." He turned eastward. "Great powers of the east, powers of birth, youth, the rising sun, knowledge and learning, hear me now." He turned to the south. "South powers, hear me now, you powers of warmth and summer and food and abundance and plenty." He turned west. "West powers, powers of the spirit world, powers of thunder and coming weather, and powers of all that is unknown, hear me now." He faced north. "North powers, hear me now, you powers of discipline and toughness and endurance, hear me now." He bent down. "And Mother Earth," he said, then turned upward, "and Great-Grandfather, I call on you to hear me now and listen to what your small son has to say.

"My grandson is a hunter now," he proclaimed, in a booming voice with a majestic sweep of his arms taking in all the directions and powers he had summoned. "My grandson is a hunter." He looked at the boy and smiled. He gently picked up the grouse, which the boy had laid beside him when they sat down.

"Brother grouse, we thank you for offering yourself to us today. You gave your life to my grandson, so that he could eat your flesh and grow strong. But you gave more than that: in offering yourself up, you made my grandson a hunter. You have given the most wonderful gift, and now you will always be remembered. We pray for your spirit, we thank you for your sacrifice, and we wish you and all your brothers to be healthy and happy and to live long on Mother Earth."

THE NONSMOKER TOOK A CIGARETTE FROM HIS POCKET (IT HAD BEEN A GIFT which could not be politely rejected), tore off the filter, and crumbled the rest in his hand, extracting the tobacco. He gave some to his grandson and took the rest in his hand. Facing east, he sprinkled a little tobacco on the ground. "Megwetch," he said, using a word for thanks from his family's native tongue. He did the same to the south, west, and north, and then to the earth as he looked down and patted the ground. Looking up to the sky, he said "Megwetch," and turning to the dead grouse, "Megwetch" one last time as he sprinkled the last of the tobacco on the ground. He turned to the growing boy and said, "My grandson, you've received a gift. It's time to make your offering in return. Do it just like I did." The boy rose and did so.

The grandfather rose to move on, and so did his grandson as the dog turned excitedly into the remaining cover. "Boy," he said, "there's a lot I haven't told you about the way that I grew up. But now, I think it's time." Slipping the grouse into the game bag on the back of his grandson's hunting coat, he said again, "Now, I think it's time. We all got a great gift today, hey?"

(Fall 1997)

A Glimpse of How It Was: The Elk Hunt

For most of history, people have known much more about where their food comes from than we do today. Only a few generations ago, most families had raised the cow, pig, or turkey that graced their tables. They cared for the hen who laid eggs, fed the cow that gave milk, picked the berries, or had hunted wild game since our mammoth-hunter ancestors emerged from the ice age.

But modern Americans are far removed from the realities of what it takes to feed people. Grain is grown, harvested, milled, and processed by unseen hands. Children are more likely to associate breakfast with the athlete or cartoon on a cereal box than they are to think of rain on a field of ripening grain. Meat rarely suggests a living animal; it comes cleaned, wrapped, and often even cooked for us. Much of our food is so fully processed that it is hard to tell exactly where—or what—it comes from.

Which is why some of my family's food these days seems so different in contrast. Our meat came from a large elk that I pursued and killed. I undertook the hunt deliberately, in part because I wanted to remind myself of the significance of food and the relationship between humans and the other living things that sustain us. I wanted to bring myself closer to the earth and the reality of what food is, where food comes from and what food means. I went hunting because I wanted to be a fully conscious participant in the circle of life, not an indifferent "consumer" in deep denial concerning the reality of food. I wanted to contemplate life and death, to experience life and death, and hopefully to make myself more aware of and thankful for both.

The elk I took was an herbivore. I spent several days becoming familiar with the country where she lived and got to know a little about the grasses she ate, the trees and the shrubs on which she browsed. I saw the sun shine and snow fall on the mountains and meadows where those plants grew, and I learned to find my way around several of the valleys and slopes that she frequented. It was tough country, and I developed a great deal of respect for what it took for Elk to sustain herself in such an area.

I saw some of the other animals with whom Elk shared her mountain habitat. Moose, standing firmly and staring resolutely as I passed by, stood in stark contrast to the mule deer who seemed nervous and jumpy most all the time. Pine martens went about their business while squirrels shuffled and chattered endlessly in the vastness of the mountain forest. Coyotes appeared from time to time, searching for food, as did golden eagles, crows, and ravens. I saw the claw marks of bears on trees and many other signs of wildlife.

I saw elk nearly every day, but mostly in quick glimpses. Then came a large herd. One lingered behind, as if to offer herself to me. I thought about the hunting partner and guide who had worked so hard to make this a successful hunt, and knew that it was time for me to do my part. I fired the shot and lived for the next two hours with the agonizing uncertainty that goes with over a mile of tracking through mountainous terrain, praying that I had not wasted life needlessly or caused injury that would be to no avail. I caught up with Elk and ended her life, relieved that it was over for her, yet shaken and sorry that I had not made it easier. I thanked her for her sacrifice and pledged that I would make sure that it would lead to good things—that she would provide good food to good people and that her nourishment would be appreciated.

It is hard to watch death like this and to realize that one caused it. Yet to me it is important to know and see and feel the full impact of what it means to eat meat. It is important to know that food begins as other life—whether that food is meat, grain, fruit, or even the yeast that leavens our bread—and it is important to fully realize the impact of what it means to take food for one's self.

I REFLECT ON ALL THIS AT THE DINNER TABLE AS WE GIVE THANKS FOR THE food that will nourish our bodies and sustain our lives. How grateful I am that Elk's life was given so that my family and I could eat. How amazing it is to see the interconnection of all things made manifest as, to paraphrase another writer, in a very literal sense I become Elk and Elk becomes me. How thankful I am as I see that Elk nourishes my son and helps him to grow strong and healthy. Thank you, I think, to Elk and to Providence for making my son so strong. I could not feed him myself and so am grateful for grain from the earth and fruit from the trees and meat from Elk and others.

I am glad that this is not just a typical store-bought piece of wrapped and processed meat—I might give little or no thought to where it came from or to the life that was given up in order for us to eat. There is no spirit, no feeling in that. Instead, I think of Elk. I think of where she lived and of the many others of her kind who remain there. I say a silent prayer that they may thrive and always be there, for their own sake and for the sake of nature—for the sake of the endless cycle of being that makes it both necessary and sufficient that sun grows plants, Elk eats plants and Elk feeds others, like mountain lion, coyote, bear, and me. I feel close to Elk, to the mountains and to the others who inhabit the wilderness. And I feel connected to thousands of generations of people, reaching back to the very dawn of human existence itself, who have hunted and eaten and prayed silently for the continued health of the animals who give us life and food.

And so I become Elk and Elk becomes me. My son becomes Elk, and Elk becomes him. My wife and those who share our table become Elk, as she sustains us and gives us life. The spirit of Elk remains with me, as does the tangible connection she provides with the reality of the American wilderness. Her death becomes our life in the most literal sense, and through my knowledge and involvement in it all I become more mindful, more grateful, and more consciously connected to the earth and the wondrous cycle of being that we call Nature.

(Winter 1998)

PART 4

Government

Northern Winter Stream

Government, Regulations, and Politics

Environmental politics. Not since the original Earth Day in 1970, when I first became seriously involved in the field of environmental conservation, has there been so much in the news about environmental laws and the controversies that surround them. Decisions are being made by Congress, the administration, and a number of state legislatures that have a great impact on the approach we will take toward the environment in general and for many very specific natural resource programs.

If you are expecting this old Earth Day activist to register shrill cries for adherence to an environmental orthodoxy built around regulations, centralized resource management, and the same view of the environment that we had in 1970, get ready for a disappointment. I'm pleased to be able to say that one of the things that has changed since the first Earth Day is that I'm now pursuing conservation work through an organization that has what I would describe as a very big tent. There's room for everyone under that tent—whether you like federal regulations or oppose them; whether you hunt or oppose hunting; whether you're a Republican, Democrat, independent, or whatever else.

Feel how you want to feel about nuclear power. Decide for yourself where the lines should be drawn between state and federal natural resource jurisdictions. Form your own conclusions about zoning and such local issues as highway projects, the proliferation of Walmarts, and other issues. It's not that these issues aren't important—far from it. People must be encouraged to speak out on them, to carefully consider and then vigorously pursue their positions through the most appropriate means, whether it is the ballot box, the interest group, letter writing, or even (gulp!) talk radio. As far as our land conservancy is concerned, the more people who express their views, the better.

But underneath our tent, things are different. We are united around one important set of principles, shared by people who hold a great diversity of views on other matters. We believe in private property. We believe in working with private owners to protect what they like about their land, and we believe in working collectively to acquire and manage land that will help to protect the scenic beauty and natural integrity of our area. We believe in an appropriate balance between development and preservation. Finally, we believe in making our land available to people for use and enjoyment—with one of the most important uses being the critical job of teaching young schoolchildren about science and nature.

Our board of trustees includes distinguished environmentalists, builders, scientists, developers, professionals, resorters, born-and-bred locals, real estate agents, and more—a typical cross section of our community. They're people with many diverse opinions on a number of issues, but they all agree on one thing: the importance and appropriateness of private land conservation. When we meet as the Little Traverse Conservancy, we concentrate on areas of agreement, leaving the matters on which we differ at the door.

For me, this emphasis on areas of agreement makes the land conservancy movement a ray of light in a public policy landscape darkened by the smoke of too many battles and an atmosphere fouled by too many oversimplified characterizations of the "other side" in terms that interested citizens, responsible corporate officers, and involved public officials should not be hurling at one another. We look for the common ground and accentuate the positive. To me, this approach represents the greatest hope that we will be able to one day rise above the politics of division. I spent a lot of time working in the old "warfare" mentality in environmental policy and, frankly, I look forward to the day when we will speak more of finding common threads than we will of pitched battles among interest groups. Such battles produce a few winners, but most end up as casualties or at best mere survivors. I believe that there are ways to create more winners and fewer casualties, and the land conservancy approach is one of those ways.

There are no litmus tests to which you'll be subjected and there's no orthodoxy to be imposed on you. We're a very diverse group, and our board, staff, and membership hold some very diverse views. We like that. It shows that we are a true coalition, built around an idea that appeals to a great many people with a great many views on other issues. Our strength comes from the strength of the central idea that binds us, not from any other source.

THE DEBATES IN CONGRESS AND THE VARIOUS STATEHOUSES ARE IMPORTANT. But to us, it's nice to know that above the din of special interests battling it out to get things their way, a few of us are busy out in the hinterlands working across party lines and across the lines that separate many other interests and groups to carry out some important work that we can all agree is right: the work of protecting what we love about our own communities, with our own money, following our own plan in order to provide our children and theirs and theirs and theirs with a conservation legacy that blends in with the developed community, adding beauty and value to an area we all have come to love.

(1999)

Government Wetland Protection

PUBLICITY OVER WETLAND REGULATION IN NORTHERN MICHIGAN BROUGHT to mind the whole question of government's role in regulating private activity and land use. While our local land conservancy takes no position on regulatory programs, of course, staff members and trustees often discuss and ponder, on an informal basis, the questions and issues involved.

In the interest of playing devil's advocate on government regulation while advocating for land trusts, I would venture this: Speaking of government protection for wetlands is about like talking about the proverbial fox guarding the chicken coop. It may rankle a few feathers here and there, but the truth about wetlands is that government—federal, state, and local—has been the number one despoiler of wetlands in the United States.

Okay, I'm admittedly biased. It has been said that no one opposes smoking more than an ex-smoker, or drinking more than a recovering alcoholic, so perhaps it should come as no surprise that as a former government bureaucrat, I hate bureaucracy.

Example: The Bureau of Reclamation so throttled our western rivers that the great Colorado, though it created the Grand Canyon, no longer reaches the ocean. The Columbia River system has been so dammed by government power agencies that entire species of Pacific salmon and trout are endangered, and fisheries are decimated clear upstream into Idaho and Montana.

The Corps of Engineers has channelized streams, drained swamps, and initiated "flood control" projects on so many acres that entire ecosystems have been wiped out, huge populations of waterfowl eliminated, and thousands of acres of alluvial farmland destroyed. Government funds the rebuilding of structures in flood-prone areas, too, through misguided programs.

CLOSER TO HOME, LOCAL DRAIN COMMISSIONS HAVE RUN ROUGHSHOD OVER the wetland landscape, eliminating entire marsh systems, potholes, pocket wetlands, and swamps in the name of progress. The most black-hearted, mean-spirited, greedy industrialist in human history could not hope to match the abysmal record of government when it comes to destroying our nation's irreplaceable wetland resources.

Today, many expect government to use its regulatory powers to save wetlands from development. Though most of the damage already done has been done by government through the aforementioned drain commissions, channelization, and "reclamation" projects, some optimists hold out hope today that government can be the prime protector of what it has not ruined already. I would be cautious here and advise, "Don't hold your breath."

It goes without saying that the above summary shows the darker side of government action. To be fair, we must look at all the positives, too: we have a wonderful national park system, national wildlife refuges, and many state, local and municipal natural lands. The Environmental Protection Agency has been created to counteract the worst works of the Bureau of Reclamation and Corps. We've made progress in teaching government bureaucracies that wetlands are important and must be spared; we've even created some new bureaucracies oriented toward protecting wetlands. And government has been used by hunters and anglers to collect voluntarily self-imposed taxes on sporting equipment that have been used to purchase millions of acres of wetlands. But government works slowly, changes slowly, and in my estimation there is reason to question whether it is appropriate to leave the entire question of wetland protection up to government.

Private protection of wetlands, on the other hand, is growing at an unprecedented rate in our country. Longtime active groups like Ducks Unlimited and the Nature Conservancy have put their money where their mouth is for decades, racking up an impressive list of accomplishments. Local land trusts—nearly one thousand in existence to date and still growing—are also making a positive difference in preserving community wetlands all over our blighted landscape.

OF COURSE, GOVERNMENT MUST CONTINUE TO WRESTLE WITH THESE QUES-
tions and devise better ways of dealing with the issue. But isn't it interesting
to note that as all the heat focuses on regulatory wetland controls, there's no
great outcry against the progress being made by the private sector? Rarely does
anyone condemn individuals who contribute their own hard-earned dollars to
their local land trust, to Ducks Unlimited, or to the Nature Conservancy in order
to protect wetlands in their own back yards or in important waterfowl areas.
Headlines don't call for changes in the ability of individual Americans to take
up a cause that is important to them and make a permanent difference in their
communities. And isn't it also noteworthy that people are supporting the land
trust movement—the private sector in land conservation—in unprecedented
numbers even in these uncertain economic times?

Regardless of how you feel about government regulation of wetlands,
you can feel good about the fact that private land trusts or conservancies are
working hard to protect wetlands without direct intervention from any level of
government. The marketplace, the goodwill of interested people, and the spirit
of community self-help are the basic tools of the private conservationist's trade,
and the tools work well.

A hundred years from now, people will still no doubt be arguing about
government's policies toward wetlands and other critical natural resource issues.
There will be learned and worthy views on both sides of the debate. But in the
background, I have a feeling that people will still be working on their own to
protect what is important to them—not because it is identified on government
lists or selected based upon some bureaucratic regulatory cookbook, but because
people have always cared about the land around them and they always will.
The private conservation movement will continue to give people the ability to
translate their caring into positive, permanent action. Our grandchildren, still
debating the government's role in things long after we're gone, will thank us for
putting some money aside to protect what's important to us and to them.

(1999)

Property Taxes

Property tax reform was a hot topic in Michigan when Proposal A (a ballot proposal that changed school funding in Michigan) won passage a few years back, and though the general furor has diminished somewhat, the subject remains quite warm to the touch. Resort property owners question the new practice of taxing seasonal residences at a substantially higher level than "homestead" property. Why, cottage owners ask, should they be forced to pay more in taxes when they cannot vote in the local jurisdictions where their seasonal homes are located and when they demand much less in local governmental services than the year-round property owners who pay less? After all, they argue, they aren't around as much as the locals to create wear and tear on the roads, they don't send any children to school, and much of the time they aren't even here.

Another concern has to do with the fact that property taxes are levied in part based upon the financial value of the property involved. Taxpayers ask why payments to support local government services and schools are based upon market value of property. Is the dollar value of property connected in any meaningful way with the cost of providing roads, schools, police protection, and other services? Does it really cost much more to provide roads, schools, or fire and police protection for a new $700,000 house than it does for a double-wide trailer home?

The point about value has proved especially troubling to me since my visit with a couple who own property on one of our region's beautiful inland lakes. This particular couple could not be considered wealthy except that they own over three hundred feet of waterfront property, acquired years ago when prices were more affordable. Though they only have a modest cabin on the land (they built the place themselves, it is small, and electricity was just installed two years ago) they are required to pay over $10,000 each year in property taxes. The couple is retired on a fixed income and can no longer afford this amount, so they are considering selling the property.

How sad, I thought, that our property tax system forces these people of modest means to give up an incredibly beautiful piece of family land in the North Country. Even sadder is that our system requires that someone be wealthy to retain an attractive piece of property.

Another complaint I've heard about our property tax system is that there is a "marriage penalty" built into the current structure. This is something I've experienced myself, as my wife and I own two houses here in Emmet County—our home plus a seasonal retreat on the Lake Michigan shore which is not habitable in the wintertime. We can claim only one of them as homestead property subject to lower rates, while if we were single or divorced each of us could claim one house as homestead.

At this point, readers may wonder what the point is of discussing the property tax system in an essay about land conservation. Rest assured, it's not to complain about high taxes on my second home. To me, the most important point is that the property tax system has a number of far-reaching influences on land development patterns, creating more challenges for land conservation than many people realize.

PROPERTY TAXES BRING ABOUT A GREAT DEAL OF LAND TRANSFER. HUNDREDS of resort cottages, farms, hunting camps, and other properties in Michigan are sold or broken up each year because the owners can no longer afford to pay the taxes. This has a significant impact on land fragmentation and development patterns. In addition, there is a significant socioeconomic impact because the land tends to migrate from people of lesser wealth to those of greater means. This accelerates the perennial problem of the rich getting richer and the poor getting poorer.

Our property tax system is in many ways a relic from a bygone era. When this system evolved, the prevailing wisdom about land was that there was plenty of it and that it should be brought into production as soon as possible. The idea that land would gradually progress from less intensive to more intensive uses was accepted as a good thing. For people interested in having a little piece of property on a lake somewhere, there were plenty of places to go where land was cheap and natural areas plentiful.

Today, things are different. The frontier is long gone. We know that land is a finite resource. We also know that natural land and farmland are important for a variety of reasons. Economically, with more and more people squeezing onto a limited amount of land, we know that real estate values are skyrocketing. It is obvious, then, that unless our system is changed, ownership of large parcels of land or valuable smaller parcels such as lakefront property will become impossible for people with modest incomes, even though the property may come to them by means of family inheritance. This may not be a deliberate goal of our property tax system, but it is most definitely one of its principal effects.

Another effect of this system is that land becomes more a commodity for economic barter than a resource for care and stewardship. Economic land use decisions based upon outdated systems are a poor substitute for land use decisions grounded in sound resource management.

There is no conspiracy to place good real estate beyond the economic reach of people like the couple I mentioned at the beginning of this column, or to penalize my wife and me for staying married, but it is happening nonetheless. There may be no deliberate strategy of using the property tax system to cut up large parcels of land or ruin its conservation values, but the outcome is obvious for all to see. Other government policies, well intended in their day, contribute further toward land fragmentation and sprawl development. One need looks no further than government subsidies for roads, utilities, and other infrastructure to see that our twenty-first-century land base is threatened by a nineteenth-century political and economic system that continues to have serious and often negative impacts on our land and people.

(Summer 1998)

The Value of Public Land

A long-simmering debate about public land boiled up in Michigan not long ago, with some rural politicians and businesspeople claiming that there is too much public land and that it's time to stop acquiring more. Some even advocated liquidation of public landholdings.

Public land stifles commerce, they complain, and limits the "tax base" in their jurisdictions. I've heard the lament since I was a kid growing up in Michigan's Upper Peninsula: "We need more tax base." Nothing is said about land, nothing about forests and wildlife and rivers and lakes and healthy places for children to grow up and families to have outdoor adventures, just "tax base," a camouflaged term for sending more money to the government. It is conveniently omitted that our supposedly excessive public landholdings in Michigan amount to less than half an acre per person.

The tax base advocates are out of touch. A lot of people in this country are fed up with the view of government as a growth industry whose duty is to find more ways to collect more money in taxes from the people. Local taxes were created to pay for local services, and wild land requires very little in local services. Study after careful study has shown that land development as generally practiced in our country does not lead to cheaper public services but instead raises the costs of those services to the taxpayers who are footing the bills.

But the tax base argument pales in comparison to the overriding significance of large public landholdings to the people of our state and nation. Here is the greater significance: that we, the people who have shaped the nation that is America, have also been shaped by the land that is America. The unique quality which we describe as the American Character developed because the story of our people and culture unfolded in a vast, powerful, and beautiful land.

This spirit stretches back to the days of American Indian culture, long before European settlers came on the scene. Indian ways figured prominently in the development of our character, culture, economy, and government. Popular examples include the Thanksgiving holiday, trade in such commodities as corn and tobacco, and key aspects of our governmental system adapted from the Iroquois Nation.

LATER CAME THE IMMIGRANTS AND PIONEERS. ASK ALMOST ANYONE AROUND the world about American culture and character, and sooner or later there will be a reference to the wilderness scouts, mountain men, and cowboys who developed their unique spirit in this rugged land. Or the "prairie wives" who provided for their families and themselves in almost impossible conditions. Or freed slaves struggling to make their way in this land, or legions of immigrants who had the grit to make it—and many who didn't and died in the attempt. The stereotype is that of a rugged people creating a new way of life against a striking wilderness backdrop which provided the context for everything these remarkable people did.

Today, there is great concern about the degeneration of the American character. Poverty, urban decay, moral decline, spiritual crisis, dependency, and other terms are all bandied about in the popular media to describe something that people increasingly find missing in America and Americans today. It is no coincidence, in my view, that these problems have increased exponentially as we have become more urbanized and further removed from living close to the land.

Most of us are no longer hunters or farmers. The frontiers of exploration have now moved into outer space and the depths of the oceans—areas that are impossible to reach for most Americans. But the frontiers of character and culture and individual progress are still within us. Cultural alarms are sounding because the tough discipline that was forced on our ancestors by the land and by nature is no longer forced on us. Technology has liberated us from the physical limitations of living close to the land, and our abundant wealth has turned discipline and delayed gratification into choices rather than conditions that are imposed upon us. We suffer under the luxurious illusion of being able to exist without discipline, without character, without the spirit that bound our ancestors together. With this has developed the illusion that we can also live without wild land. Yet our science tells us we cannot live without wild land, just as our cultural indicators tell us that we cannot live without the discipline and character which the land helped to impart upon our ancestors.

SO WHAT WILL WE DO? IT HAS ALWAYS BEEN THE BIRTHRIGHT OF AMERICANS, whether they choose to exercise it or not, to hunt and fish and explore large areas of wild land as our ancestors did. But we will only be able to maintain this birthright if we maintain large areas of wild land. If we sacrifice this birthright, we sacrifice a great deal of what it means to be American. It amounts to selling our spirit to the devil of short-term gains represented by so many shining coins and fluttering dollar bills.

The frontier is gone. There is no more wild country to explore and exploit. We must carefully manage and protect our relatively few remaining large areas of wild country, or we will lose them. That makes it especially ironic that although the frontier is long gone, many politicians act as though the supply of land and resources is endless. Shortsighted political types and scheming "entrepreneurs" conspire to convert what's left of our heritage to their private gain, leaving future generations to pay the tab—or go without. And through it all, most of us sit idly by as our American heritage dissolves, acre by acre, into subdivisions, strip malls, and a culture that gladly trades its natural capital for cars, clothes, and cellular telephones.

Sure, we need subdivisions and shopping centers. But we also need to plan for growth intelligently and allow ourselves to maintain the large land base that shaped our ancestors and makes us what we are. The watchword for the twenty-first century must be the converse of the wisdom that prevailed in the nineteenth: instead of conquering the land so that we can carefully husband our crops, livestock, and limited human population, we need to instead husband our limited land base and protect it from the ravages inflicted all too easily by a third of a billion people and technological capabilities that our nineteenth-century forebears could never imagine. We must control our own growth so that we do not destroy what's left of the land that shaped us and sustains both us and that elusive, yet precious commodity we call the American Character.

The private conservation movement, represented by Little Traverse Conservancy and others, has a key role to play in keeping nature close at hand to remind us all who we are and from whence we came. But just as it took the Northwest Ordinance and Jefferson's Louisiana Purchase to open the American West, it will take state and federal action to maintain opportunities for our children and grandchildren to wander the fringes or the heart of the Great Wilds and discover for themselves what really shaped this country.

There is hope, but it will take new leadership to shift the emphasis of American expansion from the conquest of land to the new frontiers of the information age. For though the land available for us to conquer is clearly limited, we have developed exciting horizons in technology and information-handling which offer once again the tantalizing promise of unlimited, unending growth.

THE NEW CHALLENGE IS TO GUIDE AN URBANIZED SOCIETY TO A SUSTAINABLE future without selling off the irreplaceable connection we have with our past, our heritage, and our character: the land. Consolidate public lands? Sure. Rationalize the boundaries and blend large tracts of public land in with our towns, cities and rural settlements? Of course. But give in to the shortsighted notion that there's "too much public land" and sell or give away all that remains of traditional America, and with it our children's only hope of experiencing what it was that made this nation so unique and its people so resilient? Never!

We don't have a problem of too much public land in this country; in fact, our public land base represents one of the few opportunities we have for hanging on to that special something that made America unique and gave Americans a wealth not only of material resources, but of character as well. We can do a better job of managing our public lands, but let us never forget that if we take the spirit of unfettered freedom away from the land, we will take it away from ourselves and all the generations who will follow us.

(Spring 1996)

PART 5

Economics

The Beach at Good Hart

The Natural Resources Sector
of the Economy

SINCE ARGUING AS AN EARTH DAY ACTIVIST IN THE EARLY 1970S THAT ECO-
nomics and environmental protection are mutually exclusive, my views have
changed quite a bit. Though it was dogma to many of us that environmentalism
was right and economics was wrong, by the mid-1970s, I was studying resource
economics in graduate school. In the 1980s, I began work in the private sector
of the conservation movement, using donated monies to buy and protect land.
And through those and other experiences I have learned not only that economics
is important to environmental conservation, but also that economic analysis
proves that much of what we advocated concerning the need to protect our
environment is absolutely correct. And I have come to the conclusion that
our rejection of economics said more about our beliefs than it did about the
environment or economics.

But the connection between economics and conservation is critical, especially in the area of land conservation. The key is that just as economics is
important to land conservation, land conservation is important to our economy.

Land conservation values are often referred to as intangible, but I believe it is
important to dispel that notion. Consider the various sectors of our economy as
discussed in many economics texts. There's the industrial sector, involved in the
manufacturing of goods. Fairly easily understood, the industrial or manufacturing
sector includes those businesses that fabricate or assemble goods for consumers.
Then there's the retail sector—the merchants who sell goods to residents and
visitors. In a resort economy such as we have in northwestern Lower Michigan,
the retail sector is very important. There's the service sector, too—businesses
that provide services, from car washes to catering, from window cleaning to
auto repair. Also, there are the hotels, inns, and rental condominiums that house
visitors in our area.

All of these fall into the conventional order of a local economy, but to me
there seems to be a large, gaping hole. Though this view of our economy takes

into account many of the businesses that thrive because this area is so popular as a resort and tourist destination, it ignores the very foundation of that popularity—the abundant natural resources that make the area so special.

I propose, therefore, that we give greater consideration in the future to the natural resources sector. This sector includes the parks and playgrounds people enjoy. It includes clean water, healthy air, and beautiful scenic views. It includes the deer spotted from the car window, the eagle seen flying overhead, or the fish in the creel at the end of a day's angling. It includes all those things that are traditionally written off as "intangible" but which are not intangible at all; in a resort economy they are quite literally the source of our livelihoods.

Because the natural resources sector is so important to our economic livelihood here (to say nothing of the aesthetic and other values), it is important that we consider natural resources as being just as worthy of investment as any other sector in our economy. If we pour millions into housing, manufacturing, retail businesses, or any other sector of the local economy, we must realize that corresponding investments in natural land must be made in order to keep the balance that our community and any healthy economy needs.

And balance is critical in economics. Balanced budgets are only part of the equation—balanced community economics are equally critical. We've all seen the disastrous consequences of the obsolescence of manufacturing plants in what is now known as the nation's Rust Belt. Communities depending solely on manufacturing for their economic vitality have been hammered. We face the same risk if we continually develop more housing, manufacturing, retail, and service businesses in this area without setting aside corresponding amounts of natural land, parks, scenic views, and waterfront to keep pace with growth in the other sectors. The resources we depend upon for our livelihood could disappear if we're not careful. Countless other communities from Cape Cod to Carmel have realized that the time to invest in the natural resources sector is early in a community's growth and that if the level of investment in these resources does not keep pace with the other sectors of the economy, the balance can be irrevocably altered.

Other examples abound. Where people ignore the important need to invest in the resources sector of the economy and community, it becomes more and more difficult to restore the balance that made those areas so desirable in the first place.

WE IN THE NORTH HAVE A GOOD HEAD START ON ESTABLISHING A SYSTEM OF nature preserves, public parks, and scenic views that our children's children can inherit with pride. But the community has its work cut out for it to keep pace with the tide of growth. We must constantly remind ourselves of the important need to invest in those priceless and irreplaceable resources.

As many real estate agents say in this area, they're not making any more waterfront property, and they're not making any more scenic views. I would add that they're not making any more delicate sand dunes or any more wetlands, rivers, or habitat for endangered species, either. We, on the other hand, are making many more houses, businesses, crowded roadsides, and much more traffic.

We can counter this by increasing our efforts to preserve natural land as it becomes more scarce. We can also see to it that our level of investment in those resources keeps pace with the investment in the other sectors of our economy. Million-dollar developments have been with us for quite some time, but the billion-dollar development is here, too. The challenge is clear to us to do everything we can to maintain the balance that has made growing areas so special in the past. By working together—government, nonprofit groups, and local citizens—we can do it.

(Fall 1988)

What Is the Economy, Anyway?

At the 1996 State of the Lakes Ecosystem Conference in Windsor, Ontario, people representing science, industry, government, and many other interests from the United States and Canada gathered for three days of seminars, discussion, and what has come to be known as "networking." The theme of the conference that year was the nearshore, and I was delighted to see the conference focusing not only on traditional Great Lakes water quality issues (industrial and municipal pollution discharges, atmospheric deposition of things like DDT and mercury, etc.) but also on the impact of land use in nearshore and even inland areas. There was talk of preserving shoreline marshes, considering the difference between compact and sprawling development patterns, and other things that were much more familiar to me than the usual Great Lakes talk about things like "transport mechanisms for chlorinated hydrocarbons" and "benthic macro invertebrates." Here, at last, was something that was up my alley.

At the conclusion of the conference, I was asked to serve on a panel of conference attendees to present a brief summary of our reactions to the conference, and then respond to questions from the diverse crowd in attendance. One question in particular remains in my mind: it had to do with the economic feasibility of implementing solutions to land use problems and conflicts identified in the Great Lakes ecosystem.

I only regret that I wasn't able to more fully articulate the point that was at the center of my response: that economics and most everything related to economics is essentially a creation of the human imagination, while the Great Lakes ecosystem—and the rest of the natural world, while we're at it—arose from forces that are decidedly not produced by humanity. Economics is all in our head, while nature operates on certain principles that are, for most practical purposes, immutable.

In an era that has seen many efforts made to turn economics into a "science," it may seem like heresy to some, but the fact is that economics is merely something that people made up. The classic illustration of this is that the difference in value between water and diamonds depends to a great extent upon how thirsty one is. Markets, the value of currency, and other economic phenomena are, after all, not much more than exercises in mass psychology. Not to say that economics is not important—economic matters are very important. But if we understand that economics is largely an artificial human construct, while nature is a functioning system that runs on certain unalterable principles, we have begun to crack the shell which has long been obscuring a very important point.

That point is this: when we speak in terms of environmental issues being limited by economic realities, we've got things exactly backward. The fact is that economics, as a product of the human imagination, can basically be manipulated into doing anything we want economics to do, whereas natural processes will not yield to our whims.

Example: an oil tanker runs aground somewhere and spills thousands of gallons of oil. The catastrophe is devastating to marine life, damages property, and ruins a local fishery. It costs millions of dollars to clean up what can be cleaned up, yet the negative impacts of the spill will be felt for years. In our system, the millions spent on cleanup are added into the overall performance of the economy and are seen as creating more economic activity. The millions it costs to repair the ship are also seen positively in the economic calculus, which does not distinguish between economic activity that does good and economic activity that results from catastrophic events. Can anyone really argue that the oil spill was a "good" thing? Of course not. But, as the saying goes: after all, it's only money. The overall economy doesn't distinguish between a million dollars spent on cleanup versus the same million spent on prevention, but there's a huge difference to the natural systems affected by oil spills.

How does the oil spill example look on nature's side of the equation? First off, a lot of things are certain. Certain organisms exposed to certain amounts of the chemicals in crude oil will die, period. Oil will coat rocks with which it comes in contact, killing certain plants, algae, and other organisms. Depletion of certain food organisms will lead to the death or migration of certain other species. We can argue about whether this or that effect is good or bad, but the effects themselves are dictated by nature's laws, not ours. Clams killed by oil are dead, regardless of what anyone thinks about it being good or bad. Organisms that survive by eating clams can't get along without them, and eagles that eat the organisms which feed on clams can't eat, etc. Stimulus, response. Action, reaction. The reactions are determined by nature's complex principles and interrelationships.

Contrast that with the economy. Pollution emanating from a pipe or smoke-stack was, from the days of Adam Smith until recently, largely considered to be an "externality," irrelevant to economic equations. How convenient! In economics, if something looks like a problem, just assume it out of the equation! Try assuming something out of an ecosystem, however, and pretty soon you'll have a chain reaction on your hands and things will get wildly out of control.

In benefit-cost analyses completed by the federal government, it was not uncommon in past years to apply "multiplier factors" to certain items. This is economic talk for taking a dollar in benefits and calling it two dollars because you like it. Very convenient for getting one's project funded, but there's no equivalent in nature. One deer eats as much as one deer eats, period, and you can't double the available browse in the forest by using a calculator to multiply by two. No food, they die.

I hope that at the State of the Lakes Ecosystem Conference I pro-voked people into considering the absurdity of discussing whether or not it is "economically feasible" to protect the Great Lakes ecosystem, for example. The fact is that certain actions which affect the Great Lakes will have a profound effect on the system and the millions of humans who live around the lakes. Fish can't survive in poisoned water, no matter how we feel about it. We can only grow so much food on so many acres, even with our best agricultural technology and genetic manipulation. So, the question instead should be put this way: how can we make it economically feasible to protect the Great Lakes ecosystem? Translate this to a global scale, and we're on to something.

We need to "push our little adjust buttons," as my aunt Elsie used to say, and recognize that while nature hands out specific consequences for specific actions, our economics is something we made up and is a slave to human genius and manipulation. Let's frame the question properly and rise to the challenge of consciously evolving our economic system and our mode of economic thought to the point where protecting our natural resources and providing our people with jobs and a living are no longer in conflict. The important question all along is not whether we can afford to protect the environment, it's whether we can afford not to.

(Winter 1996)

Unlimited Growth *Can* Be Sustainable

IT WAS A MANTRA OF OURS DURING THE ENVIRONMENTAL REVOLUTION OF the 1970s that the world could simply not handle unlimited economic growth. In addition to quoting Malthus, we cited the Club of Rome study, the Ehrlichs' work on population, and many other sources as proof that there were limits to growth. This variant of environmental orthodoxy is alive and well today, as many people argue against the feasibility of unlimited growth as if it were the fabled Fountain of Youth.

While I readily agree that the physical resources of the earth are limited and therefore the ability to produce durable goods is limited, it is critical that we distinguish between growth in the use of physical resources and growth in economic terms. The former involves limits, while the latter does not necessarily need to.

How is it possible that there could be sustainable yet unlimited economic growth? Well, for starters, we need to remember that economics is totally a fabrication of the human mind. There is no such thing as "real" economics, because economic values are constructs of human thought. The prices of goods and services come about because of people's perceptions. Markets are vast psychological phenomena, dependent at any given moment on people's perceptions about the value of things. It is well known that market gyrations are driven by various real and unreal psychological factors, perceptions about current events, fashion trends, and so on.

BECAUSE THE ECONOMY IS SOMETHING WE MADE UP, WE CAN MAKE UP THE means to keep it sustainable to infinity. That might sound like a naive statement, but it also happens to be true.

The limitless potential of our economic system can perhaps be illustrated by way of a theoretical example using the computer software industry. What is computer software? Aside from a bunch of disks or tapes that can all be reused again and again, computer software is ideas: new ways of manipulating data. As computer technology improves and the information age expands, there's really no reason to believe that there's an end to the way that computer software can be adapted for various business end economic functions, not to mention games and entertainment. Thus, it is possible to conceive an infinite stream of changing computer software that can produce an unending flow of wealth with minimal consumption of earth's physical resources.

The arts represent another area of limitless economic potential. Paintings, sculpture, and other works by old masters and other well-known artists have grown astronomically in value, and there's no reason to believe that there is any end to their possible appreciation. The same goes for a number of art objects, the steady demand for a constant stream of new recorded music, and so on. As music, especially, becomes just so much more information on reusable disks and tapes, the limitless potential for new information to generate new economic activity is obvious.

There are many more sophisticated manifestations of the possibility for limitless economic growth, of course. Work done by Hunter and Amory Lovins along with Paul Hawken, reported in a 1999 *Harvard Business Review* piece, shows how enlightened corporations are adapting to new ways of doing business. For example, a carpet company abandons the old idea of selling carpet in order to go into the business of providing "floor covering services." In exchange for a monthly fee, they provide and maintain floor coverings, including the actual collection of old carpet, and remanufacturing of the same material into new.

The opportunities for new economic activities are only as limited as the human mind. As the conservation and environmental movements emerge from the 1970s and into the twenty-first century, conservationists and environmentalists need to move beyond their old environment-versus-economics orthodoxy and embrace the idea that economic potential is indeed unlimited—as is the potential for finding new and more responsible ways to manage the earth's resources.

(1999)

Elephants and Resource Economics

A VISIT TO WASHINGTON, D.C., WITH THE MICHIGAN NATURAL RESOURCES and Environmental Leadership Institute in the early 1990s took me to a couple of well-known think tanks, the hallowed halls of Congress, a White House briefing, and much talk of economics and the environment with a number of people from government, business, and industry.

The conversations were lively. Topics ranged from elephant ivory to global climate change, to economics, to politics. In the rarefied air of Washington, as typically happens, elements of economics, politics, science, and philosophy were all interwoven when discussing that somewhat mercurial creation we refer to as "public policy." What public policy is best, we ask, for promoting the soundest approaches to environmental issues, economics, and so on? Being in the land trust business, I suggested that perhaps one of the best public policies is to facilitate private action on important issues.

An interesting story about elephants, heard at one of the think tanks, may help illustrate the point. The world was outraged at the destruction of much of Africa's elephant population for the sake of harvesting too much ivory. Elephant populations were in steep decline overall and people were, rightly, scrambling to stop the slaughter. Governments, which banned poaching years ago, then banned all ivory trade. Some nations even carried out summary executions of poachers. Despite this flurry of government action, however, the killing continued. Some wondered whether the elephant species would survive very far into the next century.

Meanwhile, one nation took a different approach. In Zimbabwe, the government decided that what was needed was not more in the way of government laws and bans which were so ineffective elsewhere. The Zimbabwe government decided what is really needed is stewardship of elephants. Tribal groups in Zimbabwe were given responsibility for the well-being of elephants within their traditional territories. They were told that if they were to manage the elephant herds well and protect them, they would be entitled to harvest a certain amount of ivory and keep the proceeds. In other words, they were given a private ownership interest in the elephants and a guarantee that there will be rewards if they take good care of "their" elephants. The result? Elephant populations in Zimbabwe increased, while everywhere else on the continent, elephant numbers remained in decline.

THIS SUCCESS IN ZIMBABWE WAS GOOD NEWS. BUT THE BAD NEWS WAS THAT most of the world had banned trade in ivory without regard to the efforts of the Zimbabweans, casting a shadow over the potential for Zimbabweans to reap the rewards of protecting elephant herds. Government bans, alas, do not distinguish between ivory that came from properly managed, growing herds and that which does not. Thus, piano players and ivory lovers of the world may not be able to enjoy the benefits of a wise elephant management system even though trade in "good" ivory might actually help elephants in the long run by creating more incentives to protect them. People (and governments) who have closed their minds to the idea that any trade in ivory could be good may, ironically, seal the doom for the species by insisting on a total ban. The ban might be satisfying for political activists, but it may not be the best approach from the standpoint of the elephants' long-term prospects for survival.

In the United States, parallels can easily be found. When European settlers first came to this country, for example, there were millions of passenger pigeons and no chickens. The passenger pigeons, as native wildlife, were shared by, and in a sense "belonged" to, everyone. But when they were relentlessly pursued and slaughtered, nobody really sought to protect them. Now, the passenger pigeons are gone. Chickens, however, have prospered because people own them and look after them and benefit directly from having them. Buffalo, which similarly belonged to everyone, were driven to the brink of extinction, and it is noteworthy today that the largest buffalo herd in existence is in private hands. (The buffalo seen in the movie *Dances with Wolves* were privately owned.)

The fact that we now have millions of chickens and no passenger pigeons offers a lesson, as does the condition of the elephant population in Zimbabwe. That lesson was referred to several years ago in Garrett Hardin's famous article

"The Tragedy of the Commons." When everybody collectively owns something, nobody takes a personal interest in caring for and protecting it. When people sense that they have a private, personal stake in something, however, they take care of it.

LAND TRUSTS REPRESENT AN INTERESTING PRIVATE ACTIVITY THAT RECOGnizes that people can accomplish more than government often can by taking a private and personal interest in land protection. Working with private landowners, land trusts have protected over three million acres of scenic land and habitat for threatened species.

Working to avoid the tragedy of the commons by directing private concern toward the protection of community resources is an idea whose time has obviously come. The land trust movement is the fastest-growing conservation movement in America today, and it is accomplishing a great deal. The lesson of the elephants in Zimbabwe further confirms that land trusts are on the right track—and that one of the best things government can do is facilitate private action to protect resources, and then get out of the way.

(Summer 1991)

War and Resources

IN THE RUN-UP TO THE GULF WAR, THE DISPUTES WERE ABOUT LAND. THE fact that land has been the principal issue in many of the world's wars is not surprising when one considers that land is the fundamental resource from which all wealth and food and shelter proceed. Land is the most precious commodity of all. Land represents permanence to us; land is the earth itself.

What a contrast that, as this territorial dispute raged on, our Little Traverse Conservancy celebrated its accomplishments of 1990, including more than twenty-three donations of land and conservation easements. It makes one wonder what it is that leads Americans to voluntarily give private land or rights to their land away, while battles rage in other parts of the world over the control of land. Why do Americans have land trusts and land conservancies, while other parts of the world have land wars?

I believe that the answer lies in the great American tradition of private property ownership. If individual liberty is the cornerstone of American democracy, then private property ownership is certainly the foundation upon which that cornerstone was laid. The recognition that our system of government affords to individuals' rights to own and control land is one of the key reasons why our nation has been so successful and one of the key reasons why the land trust movement has gained so much momentum in recent years.

WE LOVE MANY THINGS ABOUT LAND AND WE LOVE MANY TYPES OF LAND. From the eastern seaboard to the Great Plains, the Gulf bayou country to the Great Basin, the Rocky Mountains to the Great Lakes, we Americans love the land. We love the farms our great-grandparents homesteaded well over a century ago. We love woods and fields we roamed as children, the coverts we hunted, the lakes and ponds we fished, the summer cottage to which four generations of family have returned year after year after year. We love the land because it becomes a part of us and because we want our children to have the same adventures, picnics, hikes, hunting trips, and moments of solitude we have experienced on these beaches, dunes, forests, and fields.

Some of us love the land simply because it is ours. What originally made Americans different from their European ancestors is that they could actually own the land they loved. Although there have been instances of destruction and neglect, both the overall history and the outlook for private ownership are positive. Because of private ownership, we can act as individuals to protect our land for the future. Some of us donate our land for all to enjoy. Others protect land with conservation easements, providing substantial benefits to the public while keeping land in our families for generation after generation. And groups like the Conservancy, concerned about the future, buy land which they wish to dedicate to public use and preservation.

Nowhere else in the world have so many people given so much to the conservation cause. Nowhere else in the world do people have such complete control over private land, yet show such a willingness to yield that control to the greater good. The world's greatest democratic experiment, the United States of America, has proven beyond doubt that by placing the greatest amount of power in the hands of the individual, the greatest return can be realized for the public good. Adam Smith's Invisible Hand is indeed at work in our nation.

So we can recognize that the nation which gave the world private property ownership also gave rise to the greatest conservation movement in the world. The nation which gives private individuals the greatest control over their land provides the world's most shining example of what can be accomplished by individual landowners motivated by their love for the land and their concern for generations yet unborn.

THE LITTLE TRAVERSE CONSERVANCY'S UNPRECEDENTED SUCCESS OVER THE years is merely a reflection of what Americans, and the American system of private property ownership and free enterprise, can accomplish. It is a tribute to the people who love the land and who work to protect the land they love on behalf of the people they love. It is a tribute to the system envisioned by the founders of the United States of America and put into practice by generations of free and enterprising people. Our success shows that freedom to own the land leads to freedom to love and protect the land—and freedom from the terrible injustice that results when individual private ownership of the land is denied.

(Spring 1991)

Tax Breaks

AN AUGUST 24, 1999, *WALL STREET JOURNAL* EDITORIAL REFERRED TO CON-servation easements as a "tax loophole for the rich," and "a monument to political correctness and to hypocrisy." Examples were cited that cast aspersions on easements given by, among others, Ted Turner and Jane Fonda in Pfeiffer Beach, California, and Robert Redford in Sundance, Utah. The editorial cites easements as "uniquely satisfying not one but *two* compelling needs of *Homo Liberalis Americanus*: the need to reduce his tax burden and the need to make a show of doing something for the environment."

Well. I suppose some wealthy liberals have indeed enjoyed tax benefits stemming from their gifts of conservation easements—after all, that's what the law allows. I know that a number of wealthy conservatives have enjoyed such benefits, too, as have some not-so-wealthy liberals, some less-well-off conservatives, and quite a number of—well, it really gets confusing here because so many people fall somewhere in between.

The point is, land conservation appeals to a broad cross section of people across America. It is terribly wrong to stereotype their motives based upon political affiliations, personal balance sheets, stock portfolios, or lack thereof. And the idea of condemning conservation easements because a few prominent, rich liberals have obtained legal tax breaks makes about as much sense as condemning parenthood because certain people get deductions for having kids. If the *Journal* has a problem with the tax code, it needn't paint conservation easements as evil incarnate—many of us would agree that substantial overhauling of the tax code should take place. But in view of the progress that has been made to establish the importance of the private, nongovernmental, nonregulatory sector in land conservation, I'm disappointed to see a paper of the *Journal*'s stature stoop to using conservation easements as a means of taking political pot shots at those whose politics might not agree with theirs.

For the record, I am a conservation easement donor, and I am neither liberal nor rich. My conservation easement is a small one, and it has no purpose other than to protect the public's view from the road that runs past my property. That road happens to be one of the most picturesque routes in Michigan, receiving more publicity each year than perhaps any other scenic drive in the Great Lakes area. I didn't take a tax break, but gave my easement because I believe that those of us who advocate for conservation and for protecting the beauty of scenic roadsides should put our money where our mouth is and do something about that of which we speak.

There are dozens of other conservation easement donors here in northern Michigan, many known personally to me, whose easement gifts have been genuinely motivated by concern for the land. The *Journal* piece, in portraying easements as a tax dodge for the idle rich who want to protect their backyards, does a great disservice to these donors. Farm families in Michigan and elsewhere are struggling to keep their land in production, in the family, and out of the hands of estate liquidators for sale to the highest bidder who cares about neither the family nor the land. Many conservation-minded landowners love the land and want to see its important natural character protected. The notion that this involves any sort of "political correctness" is just plain wrong. And make no mistake, there have been tremendous gains for the public as a result. As the Land Trust Alliance's Jean Hocker stated in her response to the *Journal* editorial, "The Tax Code itself requires that every deductible easement result in a real public benefit, including habitat, public recreation or education, scenic enjoyment of the public, and historic preservation."

Our Little Traverse Conservancy turns down far more proposed conservation easements than it accepts. Easements motivated exclusively by desire for tax breaks almost never make it through the process—because the tax breaks alone are not worth it without some underlying motivation to actually protect land. The Conservancy also works hard to overcome the notion that there is any form of political orthodoxy attached to conservation easements or land conservation in general. Our support comes from Republicans and Democrats, rich and poor, East Coast and West Coast (though the great majority come from in between), pro-nuke and anti-nuke, hunters and anti-hunters—in short, from all across the geographical, political, economic, and social spectra.

THE PEOPLE WHO HAVE DONATED CONSERVATION EASEMENTS AND WHO support land conservation are as diverse as is the population of this wonderful nation, which gave the world its most dramatic example of the power of private property ownership. Instead of falling into a morass of greed and selfishness as predicted by some, that nation rose to become an outstanding example of Adam Smith's concept of "enlightened self-interest"—and thus became a shining beacon for others around the world. Thank heaven and earth that in America, the editors of the *Wall Street Journal* are free to express their opinions and vent their political and economic frustrations; it is good to have a vigorous public debate about important issues. But even more importantly, I am thankful that America has embarked upon a course of private property ownership that offers private landowners the hope of having at least as much right to protect their land as they have to exploit it. Tax breaks or no, conservation easements are important.

(Summer 1998)

PART 6

Fathers and Sons

John and Tom Bailey

Thanks, Dad

NO ONE HAS HAD GREATER INFLUENCE ON MY LIFE THAN MY FATHER. WHEN it comes to my interests, my career, my outlook, and almost any aspect of my life at all, my father's influence stands first and foremost as my inspiration.

When I was born, my dad had been working for the Michigan Department of Conservation for about seven years. He had taken a lot of hunting and fishing trips, and I suspect that, after the one he had married, the girl closest to his heart was a certain English setter named Queen. Not that she was more fun to be with than Mom—it was just that Dad ran into her quite a few years before he met my mother.

Dad had earned his degree in wildlife management from the University of Minnesota and the rank of lieutenant in the U.S. Navy in World War II. He earned the rank of fisherman using secondhand hooks and balls of bread dough in a small creek near his hometown of Greenville, Ohio. He had become a pretty good shot with his well-worn Marlin pump 20-gauge, and he had probably forgotten more about the outdoors than I will ever know.

It was bound to be that his love of the outdoors would rub off on me. If I were to identify one thing as having the most significant impact on my life, it would be the love I have developed for the outdoors. As any outdoorsman understands, it's a difficult feeling to put into words, but it can be explained somewhat by recalling the moments that stand out from the time spent Out There.

My earliest memories are of tagging along behind my dad as he followed a dog through the cornstalks in time to see a pheasant cackling and bursting into the air. I carried one of those cornstalks as a make-believe gun and scurried to pick up Dad's empty shells as he went to pick up the birds. I've loved the smell of burned powder ever since.

After the hunt, I remember peering up to watch Dad dress those big, colorful birds. He'd show me what they'd been eating as he removed the crop, and explained that you could learn a lot about the birds' habits by studying them. We always clipped off a wing and a foot for department research, and gave the meat to Mom. Then I got a long tail feather or two to put in my hat or to make into a pen.

THAT BUDDING LOVE OF THE OUTDOORS TOOK GREATER HOLD THE FIRST TIME Dad pointed out a bald eagle to me, as it soared over a northern Lake Huron bay. Something inside me was moved that day, and I knew that the sight would stay with me, even though I was only five years old.

The feeling grew again the first time I saw a ruffed grouse thundering out of the cover—alongside my dad—and still more with the triumph of finally hitting a grouse with a shotgun and shooting my first deer. Dad taught me not only to enjoy hunting, but also the importance of reverence for the game pursued.

I remember wet dogs in the car on the way home from a fall hunt; and I vividly recall those two pintails that landed in our decoys when we weren't watching—the same two birds that flew away clean as we emptied our guns, having counted to three to give them a chance before we fired at them. I remember learning to appreciate guns and shooting, along with the smell of Hoppe's Number Nine Powder Solvent in a warm house after a cold, wet hunt. I remember trees, sky, and dirt roads. I remember looking at tracks, browse lines, and signs on the ground. I remember learning how to build a good fire, backpacking and fishing trips in different places, and a hundred trips we never took but had fun dreaming about.

Dad taught me not only about enjoying the outdoors, but about working for it, as well. I learned at an early age that a dedicated person can help make hunting better for future generations, that wild country can be set aside and that progress doesn't always have to threaten (as Aldo Leopold put it) "things natural, wild and free." I learned that we can leave the world in better shape than we found it if we really try. And I learned that lesson, I am proud to say, not through politics or business, through someone else's idea of social programs or through anything artificial but in the outdoors where things are as they should be.

Among my fondest childhood memories are those involving times that I was able to accompany my father to his work as a wildlife biologist. I can't remember which I loved most: the places we went outdoors or his office. The office, an old stone farmhouse, was shared with other Conservation Department employees who always welcomed me when I came tagging along with Dad. All the folks were friendly, but I had a special fondness for the fisheries biologist across the hall. I remember him as a big yet gentle man whose office was filled with preserved fish specimens, several aquaria, and a really cool model fish that looked normal on one side but flipped over to reveal all the internal organs in three dimensions.

I REMEMBER AN OLD CIGAR BOX, KEPT IN DAD'S BOOKCASE AND FILLED WITH wondrous treasures: two stuffed bats, a raccoon skull, a deer antler, two deer jaws, and a few other odds and ends. There was an old analog adding machine, too—it seemed to have a thousand keys on it, and for some reason it filled me with fascination and wonder.

Of course, work for a field wildlife biologist was not always confined to the office or the workday. I remember Dad coming home from work one time with a burlap bag, which stood rather unsteadily on its own by the basement stairs. Naturally, Mom asked what was in the bag. As though it were nothing out of the ordinary, Dad said, "A sandhill crane," whereupon the bird let out its call, one of the strangest sounds imaginable in the back stairway of a house. The bird had a broken wing and resided in our basement until being removed to a university bird research center.

There was the batch of raccoons we fed with baby bottles until they were big enough to get along on their own, and various other creatures, all in some state of need or disrepair. Mom also supported wildlife research by donating freezer space for deceased animals destined for study. In our house, when one asked as to the whereabouts of the ice cream, you might have heard that it is "right next to the dead owl."

But perhaps one of the greatest thrills for me was the time I got to spend in the field with Dad. He put on quite a few miles checking on wildlife habitat projects, assessing the health and size of game populations, and so on. On special occasions, when we were bouncing down a particularly deserted two-track, I was allowed to ride in the back of the department pickup truck that Dad sometimes drove while working. That was one of the biggest treats about going to work with Dad.

I also got to watch as he checked habitat improvement work at various state game areas, waterfowl floodings, and other habitat improvement projects. I also remember going out late at night to accompany him to lonely rural locations where he would autopsy road-killed deer as a part of the department's research. It was often cold, smelly work in the dark, but it was fun to be with Dad.

ONE OF THE MEMORIES THAT LINGERS FROM THOSE DAYS IS THINKING ABOUT how it must have been for Dad all alone on the job. I remember wondering what it must be like for him on the days that I didn't accompany him. This came flashing back to me one day when, at the ripe old age of nineteen, I was working as a seasonal ranger for the National Park Service at Isle Royale, an island park in northern Lake Superior. I was in my patrol boat, heading from one campground to another to check things out and make the rounds. Out of the blue, I recalled my youthful wonderings about how it must have been for my dad to work alone. I looked around at the beautiful landscape, the sky, the water, and thought about how much I enjoyed my work. A broad smile came to my face when I realized that I was experiencing the answer to my question. No words were exchanged—and at that moment, Dad was over a hundred miles away—but in spite of the physical distance, I don't know that I have ever felt closer to him.

For a time before his retirement and before I took over the Little Traverse Conservancy, Dad and I both worked for the Michigan Department of Natural Resources, as the Conservation Department had become known in the middle 1960s. With all the changes that were coming as the environmental movement gained ground, some people in the department thought it fashionable to criticize the old "moose and goose" people in the department—they figured that those "old guys" had seen their day and that the new kids on the block knew better. But they were wrong. Using their same words, I can say that I take great pride in knowing that there are a lot more geese now than there were a few years ago, thanks to the wildlife and habitat management programs my father and others put in place. And, along with a large number of other people in northern Michigan, I am proud to say that thanks to my dad's vision, hard work and the phenomenal moose translocation project which he pioneered, it is possible to see moose in many areas of Michigan's Upper Peninsula once again, just as it was in the old days.

The wildlife legacy created by my father in northern Michigan will endure for generations as the moose, wolves, and other animals flourish and thrive. The inspiration and example he provided will be with me as long as I live, will inspire my son in turn, and will accompany me into whatever awaits beyond this world.

(1987)

Conservation and the World War II Generation

THE 1950 AND 1960S HAVE BEEN CITED OVER AND OVER AGAIN AS THE HEYDAYS of conservation in Michigan and the zenith of the Michigan Department of Conservation, now the DNR. People go on and on about all that was accomplished by "those guys" who ran the department back then. There's no disputing the fact that wonderful things happened in Michigan conservation in that era.

So, what was it about "those old guys" like my father who made Michigan conservation so great? I truly believe that a significant part of the answer to that question lies in the experience these men had as soldiers, sailors, marines, and flyers in World War II. Some recognition of this unique fact is, I think, long overdue.

Many of my observations about these World War II veterans and their remarkable accomplishments for conservation took shape during the late 1970s and early 1980s when I worked as a low-level bureaucrat in the Michigan Department of Natural Resources. During that time, most of the department's principal leaders were World War II vets who had returned from war to begin or resume their careers in conservation. These men are revered and remembered today as strong leaders who refused to give in to the political and bureaucratic gamesmanship that is too common in administrative government—and in that same department—today. I had quite a few opportunities to observe these amazing men, and believe that a key factor in their generation's remarkable leadership is the fact that their schooling in both leadership and following took place for many of them literally under fire in the foxholes, ships, tanks, and planes of World War II.

The films *The Thin Red Line* and *Saving Private Ryan* have drawn moviegoers' attention to the accomplishments and sacrifices of the World War II generation, as has Tom Brokaw's book *The Greatest Generation*. Years after the Vietnam Veterans Memorial was dedicated as a focal point for remembering those who served in that conflict, Congress has finally authorized the creation of a World War II memorial on the Mall in Washington, though too late for it to be viewed by most of the veterans to whom it will be dedicated.

As the son of a World War II veteran, I want my own son and his generation to know what their grandparents went through—and about the incredible service rendered by those who remained in the States on farms, in factories, and in other support functions, producing the materiel that enabled the United States to defeat Imperial Japan and Nazi Germany in the greatest conflict of the twentieth century. But, as important as it is to remember the war and the war effort, I believe that we need to look deeper in order to understand the full impact of the World War II generation on our history, our society, and ourselves.

MY FATHER, FOR EXAMPLE, WENT FROM BEING AN OFFICER ON ONE OF THE picket ships at Okinawa during the greatest air-sea battle in history to being a wildlife biologist responsible for programs across the entire Upper Peninsula of our state. The department's now legendary director, Ralph MacMullan, was a combat veteran, as were most of the principal deputy directors, division chiefs, and program heads. These seasoned leaders had developed a lot of their knowledge about leadership as squadron commanders, bomber pilots, platoon leaders, ship's officers, and in other leadership capacities—yet all followers, at the same time, dedicated to a greater cause in wartime.

When these men resumed their lives after the war, their leadership skills and sense of duty stayed with them. Their perspective stayed with them, too, and therein, perhaps, lies one of the keys to their courageous style. These men were neither intimidated nor seduced by political threats or bureaucratic games. If a senator was angry about a decision my father had made concerning deer management in Michigan's Upper Peninsula, neither he nor his supervisor, who had served as a colonel in the artillery in World War II, was particularly intimidated by the all fuss and bluster this senator could produce. They stood together, and took turns leading. The last thing they were about to run from was some ticked-off politician who'd been in diapers while they were taking fire on German soil and dodging kamikazes in the waters off Japan.

By contrast, the newer up-and-comers who were interested in pushing these "old guys" aside were terribly vulnerable to political intimidation. For many of these younger aspiring "managers"—they didn't use the word "leaders" much—a chewing out from some politician might constitute the most frightening experience of their entire lives. The World War II guys just shook their heads.

I've been out of the Michigan DNR for well over fifteen years now, and my father has been retired even longer. But I'll never forget a conversation we had one day, when we both still worked for the outfit. Dad recalled that, in years past, he was delighted every time someone asked him what he did for a living. "I couldn't wait to tell them," he said, "I was so proud of what I did and the people I worked with." He shook his head, and said, "I'm really not that proud of it anymore."

He was right. The new generation of "managers" that took over in the late 1970s and early 1980s didn't have the guts and professionalism of their predecessors from the World War II generation. Sure, there were and are many outstanding individuals, but as a whole the new generation—including my own—doesn't measure up to the generation that had survived the Depression and won the war.

I BELIEVE THAT WE'VE FAILED, BY AND LARGE, TO UNDERSTAND THE SIGNIFI-cance of the World War II generation's leadership skills and sense of dedication to principle. Their sense of duty and mission, combined with experience in combat, in defense plants, and in programs like neighborhood recycling efforts that make today's programs seem puny by comparison, constitute a perspective on life, duty, and leadership that we succeeding generations have a hard time duplicating.

Granted, their experiences were, as they are quick to point out, forced upon them. Perhaps this is one reason we underestimate them—when asked how they could possibly have accomplished so much, they shrug and say, "We did what we had to do." My generation didn't "have to." Because our parents were so successful in creating an easier life for us, duty, discipline, and hard work don't come looking for us but represent choices we must make.

My father, though my principal mentor, was not the only one. I remember talking with another leader whose accomplishments and character I admire, the retired CEO of one of the world's largest advertising firms. I once asked him if he would mind sharing his ideas about leadership and management, gained in such a long and distinguished career. "Well," he said, "I'll give you some ideas, but I learned it more in the navy than I did in business." He had been a PT boat commander in World War II.

I'm not saying that one needs to go through a world war in order to learn about duty and leadership, nor would I argue that there are no good leaders today—there are many, and I believe we're making progress. Nonetheless, I believe we often took the leadership of the World War II generation for granted, and now that many of them are gone from our midst, we're starting to understand the depth of the void created by that generation's passing. Because we're blessed with a relatively peaceful world and prosperous nation thanks to the sacrifices they made, we have to work harder than we otherwise might to become as strong, as sure, as focused, and as forthright as they.

The dedication of the World War II Memorial on the Mall in Washington, D.C., is long overdue. So is a recognition of the accomplishments, in conservation and many other fields, of millions of former soldiers, sailors, marines, flyers, defense workers, farmers, and others whose toughness and ability to rise to the call, to lead and follow, have been taken for granted for far too long.

(January 1999)

Another Generation

I WAS BORN SOME NINE YEARS AFTER THE END OF WORLD WAR II, BUT TO MY own son, I seem ancient enough to date back to the dawn of time and the early cretaceous period. But, like my father, I have taken my son to work with me on a few occasions.

One thing that can get John interested in going to work with me is an airplane trip to Beaver Island. He first journeyed to the island with me for the dedication of a new nature preserve a few years back, and when I mentioned a year later that I had a meeting on the island scheduled for a Saturday when his mother would be out of town, John jumped at the chance to go along.

The trip was more fun with John along. Instead of just sitting at the airport waiting for our plane, we headed outside each time a plane took off or landed— just because it's fun to watch airplanes come and go. We enjoyed the flight over, spotting seagulls from the air, and noticing a freighter far out in Lake Michigan. Then there was the walk we took around the Little Sand Bay Nature Preserve with Conservancy board member Marilyn Damstra, who was kind enough to meet us at the airport. ("She's nice," John announced.) "Remember when we saw the snake," he asked, recalling the garter snake we found just after the preserve dedication the previous year, draped on a stump with a fat lump just behind its head indicating recent consumption of a mouse or frog.

There were no snakes out on this cold October day, so John found other things of interest. At first he protested taking the long way back, but eventually he enjoyed it. Every overhanging branch that could possibly have been in our way was held aloft or aside by a forked stick that he had found in the woods. Several times, Marilyn and I paused while John lifted an offending branch and made sure that the way was clear to proceed.

It was a typical late autumn day, cold and threatening rain, but we received the typical warm Beaver Island welcome. As we arrived a couple of minutes late for the meeting, several of the island steering committee members remarked that they were glad to finally meet John, about whom they had read from time to time in my column in the Little Traverse Conservancy's newsletter.

As the meeting got under way, I made sure that John had the book that we had brought and his electronic Game Boy with the sound turned off. (We had discussed the importance of keeping quiet while Dad's meeting was going on.) It all seemed to be going fairly well until I noticed, in the middle of my report on some issue or another, that several of the participants were breaking out in smiles and another seemed to be making quite a losing effort to suppress laughter.

Since we weren't discussing anything particularly humorous, I cast a furtive glance over in John's direction and saw that he had ducked his head inside his jacket, zipped it up, and was waving his hands about like the Headless Horsemen of song and story. I recall that I said something to him about settling down, and struggled to maintain my composure and continue the report. John submerged another time or two into his jacket, after which he began making some sort of noise—perhaps sports car noises, as he was looking at a Ferrari in the pages of his book. Unbeknownst to me, during the meeting he had also consumed almost an entire quart bottle of Gatorade or a similar concoction, so the meeting ended abruptly with an urgent rush to find the bathroom. I wondered if our Beaver Island meetings will ever be the same.

After a delightful lunch with Marilyn and a quick trip through another of the Conservancy's preserves, it was time to head back to the mainland. On the way home, John said that he had had a great time on Beaver Island and suggested that we go out again in the summer when we could stay for a couple of days and go swimming at Little Sand Bay. I agreed that his idea was a good one. I asked why it had occurred to him to zip the jacket up over his head and was told, with a shrug, "It was cold in that room. I was trying to keep warm."

On the drive home from the airport John cranked his seat back and fell sound asleep, leaving me to reflect on the similarities and contrasts between this day and the times I accompanied my own father to work. There were no such things as computer games in my childhood days, and I doubt that a ride in a pickup truck will ever be much of a thrill for John as it was for me. But the people involved in conservation are just as friendly, open, and understanding today as they were when I was a boy tagging along with my own dad, and wild country and wildlife are as interesting now as they ever were.

I can only guess at what John will recall as the highlights of these visits to work with his dad. But I am thankful, despite the occasional exasperating moments, that I have had the chance to share a little bit of my working life with my son.

(Winter 1997)

Enjoying the Snow

HOW QUICKLY OUR CHILDREN GROW UP! WHILE CONTEMPLATING THE EIGHT-year-old sleeping on the seat beside me, I thought back to earlier days we spent outdoors together. I was suddenly transported back in time to an early winter day.

"Let's get our snow shovels, Dad," cries John, and with that we're out the door. Falling flakes sting our faces, new snow crunches under our boots, and the November gale roars in our ears. Trees around our woodland home gyrate wildly in the storm, breaking enough of the wind so that at ground level we are not so heavily assaulted by the relentless blast.

"Come on, Dad, let's shovel over here," John cries in his two-and-a-half-year-old voice. (He hasn't mastered the letter *L* yet, so it comes out "Wet's shovew over here.") He digs enthusiastically into the bank and then looks back to say, through a huge smile, "Isn't this fun, Dad?!"

It is fun. It's fun to be out with my son, but it's also fun to be out in a big snowstorm feeling the cold, seeing the snow, and hearing the rushing wind. Thanks to John, I don't listen to the "mature adult" voice in the back of my mind complaining that winter means hazardous driving conditions, biting cold, snow to be shoveled, slush everywhere, what do we do if the furnace quits and—"Wook, Dad, I made a snowbaw!!"

Indeed he has made a "snowbaw," which he proceeds to launch directly at my face. Dodging to the side just in time to avoid a direct hit, I clap a bit of snow between my gloves and return fire, hitting the sleeve of John's jacket and bringing forth open-mouthed, joyous laughter.

Although the sound of his laugh is quickly carried away by the gale, it seems to linger about us, filling our little patch of woods with fun. We shovel off all walks and decks, throwing a few snowballs in the process. John spots a bird in a tree—"Wook at that chickadee, Dad!"—which reminds us to be sure that the bird feeder is filled to the top with seed. We learn that it's possible to catch snowflakes on your tongue, that hands get too cold if you make a snowball with your mittens off, and that you can't ride a tricycle through seven inches of snow. We decide that the wind is singing a song to us, that snow is really, really cold, and that after a while we'd best go back inside to see what Mom's up to.

THINKING ABOUT THE WAY SO MANY PEOPLE DREAD WINTER AS WE TROOP back into the house and shed our snowy boots and coats, I realize that winter's song rings differently in each of us because of the way we hear it, not because of the magnificent song itself. The same cold may be invigorating or depressing, depending upon how we choose to feel it. The same accumulation of snow may herald good skiing, sledding, snowmen to make, or trouble driving to a meeting depending upon our priorities and our disposition.

Or winter can be both. We can acknowledge the difficulty of travel, we can double-check our home-heating systems, and we can dress a bit more warmly with all the wondrous new fibers that are available to us these days. We can then catch snowflakes on our tongues, go sledding or skiing with youthful enthusiasm, or just take a walk in the snowy woods to see how beautiful it all is. We can walk along the Lake Michigan shore and see the crashing waves and building ice as either menacing or marvelous, depending on how we choose to see it.

That's the beauty of nature's song: it comes to us pure and plain with no prejudice, bias, or slant. We can make whatever we want of it, interpreting it as our sensibilities and sensitivities allow.

Thankfully, many of us have opportunities now and then to see the beauty of nature reflected in the unblemished, unprejudiced views of a child. Worldly concerns that we have been conditioned to carry can melt away at these times, tired old responses to life's variety can be cast aside, and we can feel for the moment free, happy, and alive. We can escape the shackles of "maturity," slip the bonds of convention, and simply enjoy ourselves and the world around us. Freed from our mundane concerns, we can leap happily among the drifts instead of trudging through them, enjoy the sting of wind-driven snow on our faces instead of loathing it, and listen to the song of the North without judging it.

To leave those judgments behind us is, I believe, the secret to enjoying more of the North and more of life. Without those tired old preconditioned feelings about things, each of us is free to look out the window on a wintry day and suddenly burst into a wide and lively smile, our eyes glittering with anticipation, and say, "Wet's go out and make a great big snowbaw!"

(Winter 1991)

The Berry Patch and Food from Nature

ONE YEAR, WHEN JOHN WAS ABOUT FOUR YEARS OLD, WE HAD QUITE A BLACK-berry crop. John had become quite adept at spotting the berries hiding under the lower leaves, where his dad tended to miss them. He also knew his edible berries from those which are not. "We don't eat those, Dad," he admonished, pointing to a cluster of deadly baneberry. "They're yuck." He then put on a detailed demonstration of how he pictures a person reacting to munching on a lethal baneberry dose, complete with his best simulated throw-up sounds, gurgling, and the final, lifeless drop to the ground. I certainly won't be sampling any unknown berries after *that* demonstration.

But we do eat blackberries, along with the wild raspberries and strawberries that ripened before, with great delight. There's something especially satisfying about eating the food that nature offers during the harvest season. Throughout my life, I've enjoyed picking wild berries, morel mushrooms, or the apples my father and I used to encounter on fall hunting trips, growing on trees that were the only remaining sign of a long-abandoned farm or small settlement.

What is it about harvesting these wonderful gifts of nature that makes these morsels so special? Perhaps it is because, consciously or unconsciously, eating wild food puts us directly in touch with the fundamental truth that all of our food and sustenance come ultimately from nature and from the earth. When eating wild food in the wild, there's no "middle person" to get in the way. No packaging, no gaudy displays, no delivery trucks, warehouses, or barns; just Mother Nature.

After enjoying a few berries on the spot that memorable day, we filled a pail and proceeded inside to make a blackberry pie. As we stirred in the sugar, I wondered what it would be like to use maple sugar from our woods, instead of the refined cane or beet sugar dipped from our kitchen canister. Maybe we ought to tap a few trees next year . . .

FINALLY, THE PIE WAS MADE AND WE RETIRED, CLAD IN SPILLED FLOUR AND A few berry stains brought about by overly enthusiastic stirring, back to the berry patch to nibble a bit longer as the pie baked. We discussed important issues of the day, such as why bees seem to like blackberry patches, why berries need rain, and why many American Indian people always leave some berries, a bit of tobacco, or some other token as a gift to the plants or to the earth in thanks for what has been harvested. We looked at clouds, we listened to the rustle of a late summer breeze in the trees, and noticed tinges of color coming on here and there: unmistakable signs of the approach of fall and of the inexorable flow of the seasons. Awareness grows, even when we're not aware of it. Then, it was time to head back inside to sample our handiwork.

A pie tastes better—anything seems to taste better, to me—if you gather the ingredients yourself. I have wonderful memories of thimbleberry jam, made in my park ranger quarters on Isle Royale out in Lake Superior. Blueberry pancakes cooked to a golden brown on a hardwood fire in the central Upper Peninsula come to mind, as do rich jars of applesauce, canned right here in Emmet County and made from apples picked at an old homestead between Charlevoix and Ellsworth. Family forays in search of wild morels bring a smile to my face, and my mouth still waters when remembering the delicious flavor of a nice mess of morels, cooked to perfection on the family Coleman stove.

We're not avid collectors of wild foods, searching high and low for asparagus patches or wild-growing herbs. Entire seasons may pass by without our taking to the fields to gather the year's mushrooms, apples, or other fruits. But with berry bushes growing around the house, we gather enough to stay in touch with what it really means to gather one's food directly from nature. We are fortunate that we need not lose the opportunity to see, hear, feel, smell, and taste not only the fruits of nature but nature itself and the places from which these foods all come.

In the long run, it's not just the food itself that is so satisfying, but the sense of perspective we gain from harvesting it: the perspective that shows all of humanity and us as individuals as part of the living earth, part of the grand scheme of life, and part of the living land. A sense of belonging to a community is a basic human need, we're told, and I would say that we need to belong not only to the human communities of towns, families, workplaces, and such, but to the overall living community of the earth. Like the Indian leaving an offering in thanks for what the earth has given up, we need to have a sense of gratitude and wonder at the living system which gives us food, shelter, and life itself.

When the blackberries ripen again, John and I will be back in the berry patch once more. Maybe we'll talk, or maybe we'll just silently pick what nature offers, enjoying the colors, textures, and tastes for ourselves. Maybe we'll think consciously about being tied to the living earth, or maybe we won't—maybe it will be enough for us just to *be* so connected, without giving it any thought. Maybe our minds will be on paperwork, or Pokémon, or organizational budgets or the latest fashion craze at school. Even so, a berry or two will be left in silent thanks, not only for the gift of food, but for the better life that comes from being able to live close to the land and in touch with what nature has to offer.

(Fall 1993)

On Becoming a Military Family: Reflections on Home, Land, Security

"It's not just the kid who joins the Army, it's the whole family," wrote a friend. Our sons were close childhood buddies. Her words echo in my mind as I learn firsthand how true this is. Since my son's enlistment, I have embarked on a whole new host of adventures.

Among the more mundane of these is acquiring a new vocabulary, composed primarily of acronyms. I could not have envisioned, just a couple of years ago, that I would have conversations such as this:

"Wow, those ASUs sure are different than the old Class A's!"
"Sure are. Hey, what's your son's MOS?"

"He's Eleven-Charlie, but he's dual-MOS so he could go as an Eleven-Bravo, too."

"Either way, that blue cord sure looks good, especially at the NIM."

Huh?!? Well, as I'm learning, here's the translation: the new army service uniform (ASU) with its black coat, white shirt, and black tie is very different from the old familiar "green suit" (Class A) with green shirt and tie. One's military occupational specialty (MOS) translates roughly to "job description." An Eleven-Bravo (11-B) is a rifle infantryman, while an Eleven-Charlie (11-C) is a mortarman, who is also qualified as a rifleman. The braided blue cord on the dress uniform's right shoulder (oops, I mean on the ASU) means that the wearer is an infantryman, which is especially significant when one tours the National Infantry Museum (NIM) at Ft. Benning, Georgia.

A more significant adventure is visiting military installations. I toured the NIM after my son's graduation from fifteen weeks of grueling training at Ft. Benning. I was awed by the displays and also noted that there was a special deference shown to the soldiers wearing those blue cords. I was impressed and proud as the graduation ceremony took place on a field seeded with soil brought in from battlefields around the world, ranging from Yorktown and Gettysburg to Normandy and Iwo Jima—truly hallowed ground. I was overwhelmed with admiration for the accomplishments of my son and enormously, unabashedly proud of him.

The same friend who made the observation about family enlistment also wrote, eloquently, "Graduation is an awesome day. My heart swells and my eyes fill with tears just thinking about those days with my boys [she has three sons in the army]. I was so amazed and so proud of the young men who stood before me. Every moment of every day of their lives passed through my heart. I looked at them and thought of the day they were born, the moment I first held them. . . . Never did it cross my mind that one day they would be soldiers. So, my heart smiles warmly for you knowing what a wonderful day Graduation will be for both of you, and also knowing that you are now a military family and are a part of a more blessed entity than you could ever imagine." How true.

After graduation, my son came home for a couple of months before his scheduled deployment to Afghanistan. I ran outside, excited, as he stepped out of the car of the friend who had brought him home from the airport (in Saginaw, as the army felt that 167 miles was close enough to Petoskey—yet another lesson in military life). He stepped into our yard, looked at the trees and sky, and, with a huge smile on his face took in a deep lungful of northern Michigan air and exclaimed, "Aaaaahhhhhhhh, that smells *so* good!" He took another deep breath, nodded, and said, "Now I'm really home."

The first thing he wanted to do was go fishing. "I want to spend a whole day fishing," he said, "nothing else!" He stayed out at the cabin where he and his friends had spent so much time in their high school years and during his summers in college. Out on the land. Out among the trees. Out with the wildlife. Out There—where wildness is close at hand. He wanted to be once again outside in the North Country air, among the trees that were familiar to him, because that was what told him that he was truly home. Home.

It was especially satisfying to me that it was the familiar landscape and the scent of the North Country air that made my son feel most at home and that he wanted to go fishing. Shortly after going to work for the Little Traverse Conservancy in the mid-1980s, I had a conversation with some folks from a local lake association about the need for public access sites.

While lakefront property owners understandably have an interest in maintaining privacy and water quality on "their" lakes, I cited the example of a retired soldier who had fought in Vietnam and now wanted to take his children fishing. Unable to afford his own lakefront property, the man depended on public access sites for a place to launch a small aluminum boat and enjoy a day of fishing with his family. That image has stayed with me throughout my tenure at the Conservancy, and has served as a reminder that we all have our own reasons for protecting the natural integrity and scenic beauty of the North Country. I had no idea at the time that I would one day have a son who would enlist as a soldier in wartime. I had no idea that the places I was working to protect in northern Michigan would be places that he would think about when he was far away from home, exhausted and feeling lonely. I had no idea that it would be that way, but so it came to be. The homeland: Home, land.

The meaning of home to our soldiers is important, and we must never lose sight of what it is that makes one's homeland worth fighting for. In the American tradition, that involves our ties to the land. Most Native people trace their history and even their very origin to the land. For those of us descended from European migrants, America represented to our forebears the amazing opportunity to own land and make one's own living from the land without being subservient to a crown.

Yet even as the concept of private land matured here, America gave the world a great legacy of public land, including the world's first national park. A great network of national forests, national wildlife refuges, and other public lands grew as the conservation movement unfolded in the late nineteenth century and through the twentieth. Thus, along with a legacy of private land ownership and individual freedom, we have a rich legacy of public lands that celebrate our collective heritage. From sea to shining sea, our history as a people is intertwined with the land and celebrated in our parks and open spaces. The land is everything that the words of "America the Beautiful" say it is, and more. It is both our private property and our common legacy. Providing both sustenance and spirit to us, the land provides nourishment for our bodies even as it anchors our identity, our livelihoods, and our souls. Home, land: security.

Since becoming an army dad, I've had many opportunities to reflect on security as well as the importance of the land as home. I think of my late father, who defended our nation in World War II in the U.S. Navy. He was a veteran of the antisubmarine war in the Atlantic and the greatest air-sea battle in history, off Okinawa in the Pacific. He survived murderous kamikaze attacks and after the war returned to his roots as a hunter, angler, and lover of the outdoors to serve his entire career with the Michigan Department of Natural Resources.

When I came of age, I was surprised that he became agitated when I told him that I planned to enlist in the military. I couldn't quite understand why he wanted me to skip military service. He had served, I noted, so why shouldn't I? He searched for words for some time, but I will never forget what he said to me, finally: "The reason why I went to war was so you wouldn't have to."

Realizing that my father came to view his wartime service as enabling his then-unborn son to go to college without having to go to war, and then in peacetime to start a career and a family, I followed his wishes without question or regret. Yet I always maintained a special regard for the military and worked hard to nurture a sense of deep gratitude to all who served. I rarely missed Armed Forces Day celebrations at the Strategic Air Command base near our home. I made pilgrimages to places like Pearl Harbor. I vowed that I would never, ever forget what we owe our military, and I tried to teach my son these same things.

And then, just as my friend had written that she never, ever thought that her boys would become soldiers, I stood with tears in my eyes and pride in my heart as I watched my son march onto that hallowed field at Ft. Benning and become an American soldier and an infantryman.

The deployment to Afghanistan is looming closer, and so as all military parents do I am especially cherishing the time I spend with my son. I look with admiration on the changes that have taken place in him—the confidence he has developed, the poise, and the maturity. I think of him as the leader of his platoon and, like my friend, I look back on every day of his life. I think of all he has experienced and all that he has learned. I recall him saying, when he chose to go through the most demanding possible course of training and become an enlisted man rather than get the officer's commission that was just a couple more college terms out of reach, "Dad, if I'm going to lead enlisted men as an officer, I want to do a tour as an enlisted man first. And I want to take the toughest training that any of them could take. I don't want to ask anyone to do anything that I haven't done myself." My feelings of pride and admiration grow deeper and stronger.

My boy has grown up. He's a man now, my soldier-son. He has taken on challenges I can scarcely envision and has already passed tests of strength, endurance, and leadership that I can hardly imagine. But still, in this soldier-son of mine is a child of the land of the North. He still closes his eyes and takes in deep breaths of fresh air and exclaims, "Aaaaahhhhh!" as if he has never smelled anything so wonderful. He still picks berries and mushrooms, he fishes and hunts, hikes and camps, and enjoys the outdoors. Home to him is the land. As much as the blood we share, as much as we both cherish the memory of his mother and as much as our common heritage unites us, our love of the land also binds us together. Home, land: security.

Tom's son John Bailey served as a private first class in the Army National Guard, 125th Michigan Infantry, Bravo Company, and deployed to Afghanistan in September 2011. Following deployment, John completed his senior year and bachelor's degree at Central Michigan University. He got his honorable discharge in 2014.

(June 2011)

As the Sun Begins to Set

For a son who dearly loves his father and treasures time spent and lessons learned, it is never easy to think of one day letting go. But as we learn from nature, all things change and everything is in the process of becoming something else.

Leaves turn color in autumn, then fall to the ground and nourish the forest floor. Every beginning is followed by an end; every sunrise has its sunset. The bittersweet feeling of fall and sunset was heavy in my mind one day as I wrote a letter to my father:

Dear Dad,

I wanted to send along a copy of the first draft of my piece on the World War II generation. As I believe I mentioned on the phone to you, it was inspired by some long-held ideas that grew during my time in the DNR and which I have harbored ever since concerning the contributions of World War II veterans to the department and its leadership. I'll let you know how it takes shape as time goes on, and whether anything comes of it.

As I send along this draft opinion piece, I want to add some personal thoughts. First and foremost, I want you to know that the main inspiration for this piece was you. Your leadership in the DNR was a great inspiration to me, and even today I hear over and over again from people who appreciate the positive impact you had on the department, its people, and conservation in Michigan. I could not possibly be more proud to be your son and to be, in some small way, the one who is helping to carry on some of your legacy of leadership, service, and devotion to the conservation cause.

What it comes down to, Dad, is that you have always been and will always be my hero. I have looked up to you and admired you: as a boy having adventures along that creek in Greenville, catching fish on bread balls and raising a pig at the railroad yard; as a young man answering the call in World War II serving the navy, our country, and the cause of freedom; and as a wildlife biologist who helped make the Michigan Department of Conservation the envy of all state resource agencies. In all these roles, you have always been a great and heroic figure to me.

You've also been my hero from a closer perspective. I remember wanting to be able to cast a fishing lure like you or row a boat as you could. I remember learning about guns and shooting and hunting from you, deeply appreciating both your patience as a teacher and the trust you always placed in me to handle myself appropriately. I remember learning how to drive from you on those two-track trails in the woods, and the way you taught me how to train a dog, identify ducks, or look for deer sign. I remember learning countless other things from you, far too numerous to even begin to list here.

I remember that your voice was the first sound I heard each morning, awakening me for school. It was your voice I heard at night when I awoke in fright during a thunderstorm, or whenever I was sad or afraid. It was a reassuring and confident voice that was both strong and gentle at the same time, in just the right proportion. Whether you were reading to me as a child, making a presentation to some group about deer or wolves or moose, or just talking to me on the phone, your voice has always been a welcome, reassuring sound to me. Your voice, like you, has always been an inspiration and comfort to me. My father, my teacher, my mentor, my hero. These are some of the things your strong and steady voice has been to me over the years.

As I wrote the enclosed tribute to the generation who won the war, I wrote in tribute to you. It has been said that each one of us, in some small way, changes the universe a little bit through what we do in our lives. I believe that this is true, and I see it as especially true in your life. As one who helped to shape the outcome of the most cataclysmic conflict in history and then returned from war to take up the cause of conserving the earth that sustains all life, you are by any measure a man who has been at the center of the two most important issues of the twentieth century, and perhaps all of human history. I could not be more honored and proud to be able to call you my father.

Since you told me that you may be suffering from Alzheimer's disease, two thoughts have stayed steadily before me. The first concerns the commonly voiced, though I believe mistaken, thought that such a disease leads to some sort of diminishment or lessening of a person. I believe that this idea is wrong because there can be no diminishment of noble deeds done, service well rendered, and a life well lived. Quite the opposite: I hope that you do not have any fear of diminishment, because you will never be diminished to me or to our family, no matter what happens. Your life has had a great impact, your deeds have had great impact, and the spirit of all you have done transcends time and our common means of measuring things. The world is better off because you were here, and that can neither be lost nor diminished.

The second thought I have had is that I hope the threat of this disease will not excessively undermine your confidence. I'd hate to see the threat of this thing make you surrender anything a moment sooner than you need to. If it comes to pass and if you do have a disease that erodes your ability to do things, then there will certainly be a need to gradually let go. But I'd respectfully urge you to remember two things: first, resist it as long as you can and give up only what you need to. Second, no matter what happens, remember that it will never, ever be able to diminish your dignity or your accomplishments. Dignity comes from a lifetime of achievement and from a positive spirit that helps people and leaves the world better than before. Dignity comes from having made sure that your impact on the fate of the universe and the course of the cosmos is a positive one, however small. Your contributions have not been small. Dignity is yours, attached to you because of what you've done and who you've been. It can never be lost and need never be surrendered. Be confident and be strong; even in aging, even in decline. You are and will always remain a heroic figure, a blessing to a world that needed you, and a source of endless pride, affection, and love for your family, your friends, and your enormously grateful son.

With admiration and love,
Tom

(Fall 2001)

Fathers and Sons: Afterword

SEVERAL YEARS HAVE PASSED SINCE THE PREVIOUS PAGES WERE WRITTEN, and a lot of water has gone under the proverbial bridge. My father passed on in 2001, and my son spent most of 2012 on the front lines of the war in Afghanistan. Both my father and my son are my heroes, and around my neck I wear two military dog tags: my father's worn in World War II, and my son's from Afghanistan.

Hardly a day goes by when I don't think, at some point, "I wish I could ask Dad about that," or, "Dad would love this." He would be enormously proud of his grandson, not only for his hunting and fishing success, but for his work as the third generation of our family in conservation. How he would have loved visiting John and his fisheries work in Alaska! I think he would be proud of what I have helped to accomplish in my work, too. He would love the view across the little valley behind the house that he never visited and I think he would absolutely adore Heidi, who has brought so much love into my life after Jane's death.

And yet it wouldn't be right to wish him back after his time. It's probably good that he never had to see the September 11 terror attacks; as a survivor of kamikaze raids in the Battle of Okinawa I think it would have been especially hard for him to watch. As we learn from nature, everything has its time, and the flow of time goes on. My dad has moved on from what he had in this life and what he did here, but his spirit lives on. He is with us and thanks to his work there are moose in the UP once again, the gray wolf has made a comeback in the Great Lakes region, and there are more places to hunt and fish and camp and enjoy being Out There.

As for son John, at one point I had to travel thousands of miles to visit him in Alaska, where he worked to protect the fishery in the upper reaches of the Cook Inlet watershed. Since his return to Michigan, I have the joy of now being able to drive just twenty minutes up the road and drop in on him, his two dogs, and some twenty-four chickens. I can take paternal pride in the work he does to set rivers free in the North Country, removing dams and replacing small culverts that choke our waterways with timber bridges and larger structures that allow the waters to flow freely and the fish to move up and downstream as they once did. I love seeing the pictures he sends of fish caught and deer harvested, and even though we don't get out very often, it's great fun to head up to the gun club now and then to bust a few clays or pop a few targets—and I still admire and envy his shooting skills!

As the years go by I relate more and more to my father in his later years, even as my son's youthful adventures remind me of my own in years long past. I watch the progression of not only the seasons but the years and decades. Perhaps this is driven home most clearly when I see forests that have gone through complete cycles of succession—two and more rotations of aspen in the UP where Dad and I hunted grouse, woodcock and deer; also a lot of growth in both pines and hardwoods. I look at the U.S. and world populations of human beings, more than doubled since I was born. I consider the technology that seems to always leave me behind and remember Dad's mother, who seemed almost bewildered when men walked on the moon, saying, "I grew up in horse-and-buggy days!"

I can relate to that. I remember marveling that my grandmother knew Annie Oakley, and thinking of my father growing up in times that seemed practically ancient to me. While I try to keep up with some of the technology and change today, I let quite a bit of it simply pass by, saying, "I'm a mid-twentieth-century guy."

Age doesn't seem to bother me too much; in fact, with passing years I find myself becoming more and more content. I attribute part of this to the affection and admiration I had for my dad and uncles when I was growing up—I loved their stories of adventures and early times, and in many ways aspired to be like them with longer memories and, hopefully, accumulated wisdom. The physical aspects are not all that welcome; reading glasses are a pain, and the various aches and ailments that come with accumulating years are nothing to enjoy. Nonetheless, I feel a great sense of accomplishment and satisfaction with all the miles I've put on this body and all the things I've seen with these eyes. It has been an amazing journey. I have been abundantly blessed in this life and I am grateful beyond measure.

As for work, in a couple of years I will head into retirement with a solid feeling of accomplishment and few, if any, regrets. I've been lucky to have arrived in the right place at the right time with the right background and skills to make a positive difference. Few things can be more satisfying in life than to feel as though one is leaving the world a bit better off for one's having been here.

A lot of the credit for what I've been able to do goes to my father and my son. They both fought for my freedom. They both taught me many lessons, as only a father can teach his son and only a son can teach his father. One showed me the way into conservation work, and the other gives me hope for carrying it on after I've retired. Both have inspired and enriched my life beyond anything I could have hoped for. And so, I can observe at the end of this afterword as I did at its beginning that my father and my son are both my heroes.

(Fall 2016)

Acknowledgments

MANY PEOPLE PLAYED IMPORTANT ROLES IN BRINGING THIS BOOK ABOUT. All but a few of these essays were written for my column in the quarterly newsletter of the Little Traverse Conservancy, which has provided me with my livelihood for more than three decades. Far from being one of the people to whom Henry David Thoreau referred in his comment about people living "lives of quiet desperation," I am one of the lucky ones who has been able to earn a living doing what I love. I am deeply indebted to the Conservancy, its Board of Trustees, donors, members, and dedicated staff members for this wonderful opportunity. It has been a great pleasure for me, four times each year, to pretend that I'm a writer and produce these essays. They came through me as part of my work, they belong with that work, and so this book is not mine, but a product of the Little Traverse Conservancy. Much of this manuscript was assembled during a sabbatical that was generously given to me by the Conservancy in the 1990s. All proceeds from this book will go to the Conservancy which has given me such a wonderful life.

I am grateful to Gloria Whelan, who was the first to encourage me to assemble my essays into a book. Without her planting the seed, it never would have happened. And I am doubly grateful to her for writing the foreword to the book.

As Gloria's seed germinated, the idea was nurtured by encouragement from Mary Sojourner, whose writing has inspired me and whose personal friendship and encouragement have motivated me. She is a true sister in spirit. Lynne Walters Fraze put a lot of work into developing the manuscript, and there was help and encouragement along the way from Pam and George Houck.

Then there's Dave Dempsey. In a class by himself as a conservation historian and writer, he made me believe in this project and he helped me to believe in myself. His support and encouragement have been matched only by his tireless volunteer efforts as editor of this work, and his friendship is treasured beyond measure.

Anne Fleming of the Conservancy staff has taken time from her many other tasks to handle the many logistics of the project, and I can never thank her enough.

Marty Amiln, Heidi Marshall, and Peggy Swenor took time to proofread the manuscript and provided many helpful suggestions. I did my best to look over all three sets of comments and incorporate a sort of consensus into the final product.

To Linda and the people at Michigan State University Press, thank you so very much for all your work and support.

To all of these people, and many more who encouraged and helped me along the way, my deepest gratitude.

Beyond those named above, there are number of people who have not only worked on this book, but who played major roles in many of the essays themselves. My father, the late Ralph E. Bailey, was my first hero, my role model, my guide in life and remains a constant source of inspiration and motivation. My mother, Jean Bailey, was always my biggest supporter and always pulling for me in the background. My sister Catherine was always there for me and but for her support through trying times in youth I would not have survived intact.

My uncle, Wayne Booth, was another great mentor who introduced me to go-light backpacking and a whole new dimension of the outdoor world.

My late wife, Jane M. Bailey, loved and supported me through it all, including the time when I made the big and risky career jump from the security of civil service to a sleepy little nonprofit in a fairly remote area. She sacrificed a great deal to help me live my dream, she brought our wonderful son into the world, and she taught me profound lessons about life and love.

My son John Bailey has been many things to me, all of them precious. From the kid who reminded me of the fun one can have in a snowstorm he grew to become a warrior-defender of freedom on the front lines in a particularly difficult war, and is now a conservation professional in his own right.

Last and in no way least, Heidi Marshall did much more than provide the beautiful paintings which illustrate this book. She brought color and beauty into my life when it seemed as though things had turned grey. Through her and her son, Parker, I learned that there can be life after grief, that hope springs eternal, and that sharing life and love with the right person can be the most fulfilling experience one can have.

To all those named here, thank you. To all those others, too numerous to recognize here, I hope that you will enjoy these essays, which are written for you. Thank you.

ABOUT THE AUTHOR

Thomas C. Bailey, executive director of the Little Traverse Conservancy since late 1984, has helped the Conservancy grow from a small community organization to a nationally recognized conservation institution. The Conservancy under his leadership has created more than three hundred nature preserves, protected public values on private acreage with conservation easements, and acquired land for local parks, state parks, state forests, and national forests. His success has resulted in his being called to a number of public service positions, including four appointments by two Michigan governors as well as service on the National Land Trust Council of the Land Trust Alliance. He was cofounder of both the Top of Michigan Trails Council and the Heart of the Lakes Center for Land Conservation Policy, which serves as a coordinator, policy voice, and think tank for Michigan's land conservancies. He previously spent six years with the Michigan Department of Natural Resources and served as a national park ranger at Isle Royale National Park and Grand Portage National Monument. His involvement in conservation policy began when he first testified as a citizen activist before the US Senate Interior Committee at the age of seventeen. He also worked as a fishing guide in Michigan's Upper Peninsula, where he grew up. Tom now resides near Petoskey, Michigan.

ARTWORK

Heidi Marshall has been recognized locally as winner of several plein air painting competitions; statewide in the Gold Medal Show at Detroit's Scarab Club and an exhibition of her work at the University of Michigan; nationally as a National Park Artist in Residence and internationally through the Degas Pastel Society's nineteenth annual juried exhibition.

ABOUT THE AUTHOR OF THE FOREWORD

Gloria Whelan writes for children and adults. She has received the National Book Award, the 2017 Mark Twain Award, the Great Lakes Booksellers Award, three Michigan Notable Books Awards, Distinguished Achievement Award from the Educational Press Association of America, the silver medal in the Short Story Fiction IPPY Awards, and the National Outdoor Book Award. Her books have been printed in numerous foreign countries.